D0021501

GARDEN
BLESSINGS

Also by June Cotner

GARDEN BLESSINGS

POEMS, PROSE AND PRAYERS CELEBRATING
THE LOVE OF GARDENING

BY JUNE COTNER

Published in the United States by Viva Editions, an imprint of Cleis Press, Inc., 2246 Sixth Street, Berkeley, California 94710.

Printed in China.
Cover design: Scott Idleman/Blink
Cover photograph: Deborah Harrison/Getty Images
Text design: Frank Wiedemann
First Edition.
10 9 8 7 6 5 4 3 2 1

Trade paper ISBN: 978-1-936740-81-9
E-book ISBN: 978-1-936740-94-9

Library of Congress Cataloging-in-Publication Data

Garden blessings : poems, prose, and prayers celebrating the love of gardening / edited by June Cotner. -- First edition.
    pages cm
  ISBN 978-1-936740-81-9 (paperback)
1. Gardeners--Prayers and devotions. 2. Gardening--Poetry. 3. Self-actu-alization (Psychology) 4. English poetry. I. Cotner, June, 1950- editor of compilation.
 BL444.G37 2013
 635--dc23
                              2013041136

For Denise Marcil, my literary agent,
for always believing in the vision for this book;
and for Susan Cotner, my sister,
who is the happiest gardener I know!

Contents

Letter to Readers

"Trivial annoyances slough off in a garden and problems often solve themselves there as you weed and plant. Gardening is such satisfyingly creative work, too; you can see the beautiful results of your efforts."

—HELEN VAN PELT WILSON (1901–2003)

The quote above succinctly expresses how many of us feel about gardening. Whether it's pulling weeds or the vision of creating beauty that relieves our frustrations, most of us feel better after gardening.

Gardens are universally enjoyed and they have the unique quality of combining art and nature. Gardens are especially poetic in our daily lives as evidenced by the fact that poets write about gardens and gardening as frequently as they do above love.

Many of us have a dear relative who nurtured our love of gardening; in my case, my grandfather and I shared many relaxed times together as we puttered in the garden. Likewise, contributing poet Penny Harter has a fond remembrance of shelling peas with her mother and grandmother. Poet Michael S. Glaser is creating a new memory within his own family as he uses butternut squash from his garden to make soup for his granddaughter. Peter Markus states that his daughter Helena "is the newborn keeper of our family garden. She shall inherit more than just the earth."

In *Garden Blessings*, you will discover inspiring selections about the garden from classic writers such as Walt Whitman, Ralph Waldo Emerson, and Celia Thaxter, to contemporary writers such as Barbara Crooker, Michael S. Glaser, and Ellen Bass.

I have been compiling anthologies for twenty years now and have more than 900 contributors who send me their poems, prayers, and prose for each of my books. Because of the inclusion of so many contemporary writers, I believe you will find refreshing selections in *Garden Blessings*.

You will also find some humor in *Garden Blessings* from "My Garden's Protected" by Robin M. Svedi to "A Gardener's Lament" by Susanne Wiggins Bunch.

One little poem, which celebrates our connection to the spiritual side of gardening, has followed me around for many years. I have seen it on many garden plaques and I never tire of reading the charming words of Dorothy Frances Gurney:

The kiss of the sun for pardon,
The song of the birds for mirth,
One is nearer God's heart in a garden
Than anywhere else on earth.

I hope this book captures the creativity, spirituality, and beloved satis-
faction of gardening. I believe you are in for a treat as you read and
reflect on new poems, prayers, and prose expressing a profound love
for gardening.

JUNE COTNER

Thanks

This anthology has been in the works for more than a decade. I owe my first thanks to my longtime agent, Denise Marcil, for believing in this project for so many years; my second thanks goes to Anne Marie O'Farrell (both at Marcil-O'Farrell Literary) for helping me shape this lovely book.

My heartfelt gratitude goes to my husband, Jim Graves, and my many relatives and friends who encourage and inspire me every day.

I am thrilled to work with Brenda Knight, publisher at Viva Editions, and so appreciate her enthusiasm for *Garden Blessings*. When we first met in January 2013, Brenda noticed my book, *House Blessings*, and asked, "When are you going to do *Garden Blessings*? I love to garden!" She immediately asked for a proposal and sample selections. My unknown connection with Brenda goes back many years, which I discovered when we met. She had worked at HarperCollins and was familiar with and enthusiastic about my first anthology, *Graces* (HarperOne). She continues to use *Graces* since the time it was first published in 1994.

While the manuscript was close to complete by the time I met with Brenda, we both agreed that it would be good to solicit for more selections. I did so, and am honored to include new selections by writers such as Gayle Brandeis ("Choking" and "Avocado"), Dr. Norman Wirzba ("Spiritual Gardening"), and Jean Tupper ("Love Poem for the Gardener").

Some of my relationships with my contributors go back for twenty years and many of those same authors have been published in a number of my other collections. I have often said that I feel like a florist putting together a bouquet from abundant, beautiful flowers—and this could not be more true than it is with *Garden Blessings*.

And lastly, I'm grateful to God who brings me in touch with so many wonderful contributors without whom my anthologies would not exist.

one

THE GARDEN

A garden always gives back more than
it receives.

—MARA BEAMISH

GARDEN TALK

Gardens speak of Paradise,
of freedom,
of being yourself

Gardens say,
Slow down,
Look around you,
Believe,
Hope,
Blow away those cranky thoughts

Gardens talk—
If you are willing to listen,
And remain quiet only—
Awed by the greatness
of the music of your soul.

—ZORAIDA RIVERA MORALES

THE GARDEN IS RICH WITH DIVERSITY

The garden is rich with diversity
With plants of a hundred families
In the space between the trees
With all the colours and fragrances.
Basil, mint and lavender,
God keep my remembrance pure,
Raspberry, apple, rose,
God fill my heart with love,
Dill, anise, tansy,
Holy winds blow in me.
Rhododendron, zinnia,
May my prayer be beautiful
May my remembrance O God
     be as incense to thee
In the sacred grove of eternity
As I smell and remember
The ancient forests of earth.

—CHINOOK PSALTER

MORNING'S GIFT

Like a Pied Piper
        the sounds of early morning
                coax me out of bed
and I follow
                knowing that the morning
holds secrets
                the rest of the day will never know.
There is something relentless
                about that speck of salmon sky
                        invading the east
                                and mingling with the dark clouds
                                        on the horizon

—MOLLY SRODE

REFLECTIONS ON THE GARDEN

Half the interest of a garden is the constant exercise of the imagination.

—ALICE MORSE EARLE (1851–1911)

The scents of plants are like unseen ghosts. They sneak upon you as you round a turn in the garden, before you see the plants from which they came.

—BARBARA DAMROSCH

The great challenge for the garden designer is not to make the garden look natural, but to make the garden so that the people in it will feel natural.

—LAWRENCE HALPRIN (1916–2009)

Gardens are not created or made, they *unfold,* spiraling open like the silk petals of an evening primrose flower to reveal the ground plot of the mind and heart of the gardener and the good earth.

—WENDY JOHNSON

To share a garden is to share a lifetime, past, present, and future.... Plants that grew and bloomed in my grandma's garden now grow and bloom in my own garden.

—LAURA MARTIN

Almost any garden, if you see it at just the right moment, can be confused with paradise.

—HENRY MITCHELL

A garden is a delight to the eye, and a solace to the soul; it soothes angry passions, and produces that pleasure which is a foretaste of paradise.

—SA'DĪ, PERSIAN POET (1213–1292)

One of the most exciting things about planning a garden is the many and varied ways there are to play with color—from blending great masses of color to highlighting the gemlike glow of a single blossom.

—BARBARA DAMROSCH

A morning-glory at my window satisfies me more than the metaphysics of books.

—WALT WHITMAN (1819–1891)

IMPERMANENCE

At daybreak if the weather is fine, I go into the garden. This time of day is very special to me. The sky is clear, I see the stars, and I have this special feeling—of my insignificance in the cosmos, the realization of what we Buddhists call impermanence.

—THE DALAI LAMA

THE GARDEN HOUR

It's enough that Norway maples sway
wind-sizzled through long branches. Enough too
that violets, primrose, and the creamy peony
stretch, and trumpet vines blare their deep rue.
It's enough that the rain, April-cool,
pellets the good roof—mazurka of steam
and squirrel's feet. Ivy-lined gutters, drain pipes spool,
splash, slither down the driveway's crooked seam.
Perhaps wisdom grows unexpected as wild grapes
and paradise is a garden returned to bruised.
Yet cardinals flash their tango capes
and maples bud maroon and chartreuse.
Take hold of one more root. Breathe in fragrant flower.
Let worries cease. Embrace this garden hour.

—CHRISTINE SWANBERG

EDEN

Eden is found
in the garden
a solitary space
the source of life
hidden
beneath the earth.

Roots grabbing hold of life
a stem of strength reaching upward
buds ready to blossom
a flower opening to soak in light
fruits, herbs and vegetables ripening under
the nurturing care of the gardener.

Life springing forth
from the touch of hands
planting, pressing seeds into soil
digging, holding the dust of earth.

The slow process of growth
reminding gardeners to be patient
slow down; soak in the sun
let troubles vanish
let thoughts flow
like gentle streams
over pebbles.

Time is eternity here
in the garden where
Eden is found.

—SHERRI WAAS SHUNFENTHAL

GARDEN PROVERBS

The garden must be prepared in the soul first or else it will not flourish.

—AUTHOR UNKNOWN

Gardens are not made by singing "Oh, how beautiful," and sitting in the shade.

—RUDYARD KIPLING (1865–1936)

More grows in the garden than the gardener sows.

—SPANISH PROVERB

If you would be happy all your life—plant a garden.

—AUTHOR UNKNOWN

THE NEW GARDEN

Each day a surprise
unfurling on twig and stem,
stretching from earth into sun,
blooming in unexpected corners.
Our yard comes to life in luxurious, sweet welcome.

Next spring
we will begin to leave our mark,
changing this garden to fit our own needs and yearnings.
But for this first cycle of seasons
let us simply watch and appreciate,
thanking those who have gifted us
with a year of discovery
and beauty.

—SHARON HUDNELL

DAWN APPROACHES

As the dawn approaches
chasing away night's shadow,
dew glitters as if diamonds
sparkle across the velvet grass
A trilling song bursts forth
from a feathered throat,
greeting the brand new day
with full voiced splendor
Gentle breezes, softly whisper
among ruffled petals, opening
spreading sweet fragrant scent
with each warm breath
As I sit, quietly, peacefully,
drinking in each nuance,
quenching the deep thirst
within my very soul

—LINDA LEE RUZICKA

OASIS

Sun dappled Monarchs bask
On this spot of earth
I've transformed

The fountain water muffles
Sounds of traffic
Beyond the fence,

A barrier to my solitude.
Here I slacken
In the scented flora.

Sometimes I read,
Sometimes I dream
Here in my garden,

Serenity.

—IRENE SEDEORA

YEAR-ROUND BLESSING

It's winter but I'm at the window again,
daydreaming about my garden.

Along the sidewalk, my mind can see
yellow tulips, an early sign of spring.

Over there, savory tomatoes will grow.
I imagine their juice spilling down chins.

Hear those thumps on the grass?
Ripe red apples drop from their tree.

I ponder chrysanthemum colors for fall:
White would be pretty but so would rust.

Finest in its growing season, that garden
blooms in my heart all year long.

—JOANNE KEATON

GARDENS

Gardens are more than
hooded flowers, tempting fruits
and living trees.
They are the birds
that sing and fly in them,
the wing-eyed butterflies,
the golden bees.
They include the sky
with sun and moon and stars,
the rain and snow;
they are the earth
with captured light from heaven
where plants and people grow.
A garden is a universe
that whispers soft and vernal,
"As it is above, so it is below."

Waking, blooming, sleeping,
waking up again,
gardens are eternal:
they teach us all we need to know.

—THELMA J. PALMER

A GARDEN BLESSING

May fertile earth accept these seeds
and spare me from excessive weeds.
As plants take root and start to grow,
help me protect with rake and hoe.
Send rain to soak my precious crop
and sun to nourish from the top.
Keep bugs and rodents far away
and also hold disease at bay.
Most important, at least for some,
bless this gardener with a green thumb.

—BARBARA NUZZO

RHAPSODIES WITHIN

My garden is my refuge, I find a solace here.
I tiptoe toward the rhythm and a rhapsody I hear:
The feathered ones give concerts, it seems they all agree
That now they are together, there needs be melody.
The flowers show their colors, as blossoms come to bloom—
They outdo one another in a wonder of perfume!
Extravaganzas greet me in the most exciting ways!
My heart is ever filling with the marvelous displays!
My song is not perfected, nor is my beauty rare,
But I receive a welcome within my garden prayer.
I dance within the stirrings of the love which takes control,
And I am elevated by the flutter in my soul!

—JEANI M. PICKLESIMER

GRANDMA AND GRANDPA'S BACKYARD

they said it started as a Victory Garden
during WWII and it just
got bigger

he raised rhubarb
gooseberries
beets
lettuce
sweet corn
winter onions

and white
icicle radishes

she planted lilacs
zinnias
hollyhocks
a pink climbing rose
a yellow climbing rose
and mounds of lily-of-the-valley

the best thing was
they had no
grass

—SHERYL L. NELMS

AFFAIR IN A GARDEN

Beneath the overgrown grass swells the rich brown body
of the Earth. I want to throw myself down on it,
embrace it. I want to hug the trees, their high
summer lushness a green temptation.
Wildflowers appear, planted years ago,
flirtatiously blooming now as if they had
all the time in the world to grow
so beautiful and, of course, they do.
This is why as I bask in August sun
in the garden with perfumed breeze
stroking my bare legs and arms and face,
I am totally in love, wanting only to be
one with this pulsing planet.

—ARLENE GAY LEVINE

two

THE GARDENER

As is the gardener, so is the garden.

—PROVERB

GARDENER'S PRAYER

O Lord, grant that in some way
it may rain every day,
Say from about midnight until three o'clock
in the morning,
But, You see, it must be gentle and warm
so that it can soak in;
Grant that at the same time it would not rain on
campion, alyssum, helianthus, lavender, and others which
You in Your infinite wisdom know
are drought-loving plants—
I will write their names on a bit of paper
if you like—
And grant that the sun may shine
the whole day long,
But not everywhere (not, for instance, on the
gentian, plantain lily, and rhododendron)
and not too much;
That there may be plenty of dew and little wind,
enough worms, no lice and snails, or mildew,
and that once a week thin liquid manure and guano
may fall from heaven.
Amen.

—KAREL CAPEK (1890–1938)

GARDENING MOTHER

She kneels in the dirt,
Overcome by its fragrance,
Musty and sweet,
Nature's perfume.
She sows the seeds,
Which will grow ripe in time,
Requiring her nurture until then;
Her loving, tender care.
She is the mother of the garden,
Who watches over her crop
Careful to remove the weeds,
To fertilize, and feed,
Her bounty is rich,
Her rewards eternal.

—PAULA E. KIRMAN

REFLECTIONS ABOUT GARDENERS

The longer you garden the better the eye gets, the more tuned to how colors vibrate in different ways and what they can do to each other. You become a scientist as well as an artist, with the lines between increasingly blurred.

—MARJORIE HARRIS

The most noteworthy thing about gardeners is that they are always optimistic, always enterprising, and never satisfied. They always look forward to doing something better than they have ever done before.

—VITA SACKVILLE-WEST (1892–1962)

A small garden, accordingly, gives its owner a far greater opportunity to express himself...in a garden any man may be an artist, may experiment with all the subtleties or simplicities of line, mass, color, and composition, and taste the god-like joys of the creator.

—H. G. DWIGHT (1875–1959)

LOVE POEM FOR THE GARDENER

From my upstairs window I watch
as long fingers, green from staking tomatoes,
gather flowerets of broccoli for stirfry,
cosmos for my vase.

You'd think I'd be able to pen a few lines
for the tall one out there in the garden
in his old straw hat, frayed jeans,
and holiest tee—that gimpy left leg
outstretched, refusing to bend—
the man I've loved all these years,
now planting another row of radishes,
now loosening the earth around me.

Surely there is something I can tell
about the way he sweeps me in—
those brown eyes (deepset, green-flecked)
that listen hard and say things
he'd never say aloud. His silence
the kind that soaks up my sorrow, feeds my joy.

—JEAN TUPPER

WHY?

I turned the soil...an act of hope.
I planted the seed...an act of faith.
I carried the water...an act of sustenance.
I pulled the weeds...an act of maintenance.
I reaped the rewards...an act of thankfulness.
I shared the fruits of my labors...an act of love.
I am a gardener...because I believe.

—SANDRA E. MCBRIDE

NATURAL

My nails have no polish.
They're clipped short.
My hands are not smooth,
And lotions can't help.
Tiny clumps of dirt
Seem embedded, and
Indifferent to soaps.
Useful hands, planting,
Weeding, seeding, pinching,
Nurture my soul as well
As my garden.

—LOIS GREENE STONE

A BLESSING FOR A GARDENER

From the glowing burst of sunrise
And all the daylight through
May the beauty of the world
Be a blessing for you.

May the gentle touch of springtime
And summer's bright array
Embrace you with their cheerfulness
As they color every day.

When the sunny gold of autumn
Is brushed by winter white
May you always hold the hope
That sustains us through the night—

The hope that returning springtime
Will dawn and renew earth
As the blessings of God's goodness
Delights you in rebirth.

—THERESA MARY GRASS

THE EARTH TURNS GREEN

In the mud
On hands & knees

In the dirt
Where earthworms sleep

The gardener
Plants his seeds.

The gardener's heart
Not even weeds

Will break apart
The gardener's peace

Beneath whose knees
The earth turns green.

—PETER MARKUS

THE GARDENER

Kneeling as if in prayer, the gardener commits an act of worship, her hands running through the clumps of earth. Like so many rosary or mala beads, the dirt slips through her fingers as she chants her garden mantra: "May I help to plant the seeds of delight, nourish and water this patch of land with love, weed out discontent and witness its miraculous growth, knowing that I am the co-creator of beauty."

—REVEREND EDIE WEINSTEIN

GRANDMOTHER

Summers and summers in this garden,
and still each blossom of tomato

surprises with its skinny burst
of sun. And the squash, those

orange trumpets lazing everywhere,
leaves and tendrils sprawling across

every path I thought I'd cleared.
Beer cups, marigolds, flapping

aluminum pans on twisting cords:
who says a row of lettuce

and a line of beans can't survive?
I've worked my hands in every

crevice of this place, called forth
colors and shapes no artist's brush

could ever hope to conceive.
In my basket I carry the face

of the woman I have learned to be:
keeper of question, believer in love,

my hair a growing braided vine
beneath this bonnet of straw.

—KATHARYN HOWD MACHAN

THE OLD GARDENER

His eyes aren't what they used to be
his knees creak as he bends
but every morning with the dawn
he harvests what God sends

In early spring he planted
despite his aching hand
he tilled and seeded
one by one
as he worked and loved the land

His best years are behind him
aging takes its toll
but in the tending of the earth
the old gardener is made whole

—NANCY LYNCH GIBSON

INTO A BOUNTIFUL SEASON

Fingers caked with dark rich soil she realizes
she hasn't pulled a weed
picked a peapod off a tangled vine
or brushed the dirt from a fat, slightly deformed
naturally shaped carrot in 15 years.
She's been city living, in in-fill lots
where lawns are heavily watered in drought times
and the beets are pickled by Bicks.
But now, in this, her 40th year
she tends garden:
a neatly lined, practical assemblage of
russet potatoes, Little Marvel peas, onions
and even, persnickety corn.
She pushes in another hopeful seed.
She thinks of her mother, the farm, spiced pumpkin pie;
softly reminded by the moist cool earth of
who she is.

—CAROL L. MACKAY

A POET RETURNS TO THE GARDEN

Geese fly over head in victory
the same day a seed catalog appears.
Time to misplace this pen and grab
a shovel, scrape away winter's layers
to reveal a bare slate of soil, create
new lines of snap peas, plum tomatoes,
and Bibb lettuce. I want to plant
impatiens, Johnny-jump-ups, and unleash
explosions of pink, orange and blue.
I am itching to battle aphids, declare war
on Japanese Beetles, offer slugs one last beer.
When nature edits my plan or volunteers
her ideas, I am pleased. For months
I will dig in this fertile ground,
while my compost heap glories
in its decomposition.

—BG THURSTON

GLORY TO THE GARDENER

The gardener slowly works the soil with firm hands born of time
that instinctively caress the tired earth.
Turning over its parched surfaces that long to be quenched,
renewing its strength and fertility with an offering of love.
For the gardener has a gift
of breathing new life into the dust of seasons past,
teasing memories from its depth
and recreating former splendor from their tiny seeds.
And by the gardener's simple touch,
the miracle of life springs forth
in a burst of colors, shapes, textures, and scents,
that bring glory to that once barren soil,
and the gardener with firm hands born of time.

—HEATHER BERRY

A GARDENER KNOWS ANOTHER GARDENER

A gardener knows another gardener
When she sees jaunty stiffness in his walk
When he parks by the forsythia, not the market door
When the silken blue clematis turn their heads
                    at the same time.

A gardener knows another gardener
When she makes him tea at 6 a.m. on the porch
When he brings her shell pink roses, still potted
When they kiss and the Earth feels firm and warm
                    under their feet.

—PAMELA BURKE

BLESS THE GARDENER WHO

believes great things grow
from small beginnings

appreciates sunshine and rain
and the rhythm of the seasons

plows through troubles
willing to get hands and knees dirty

remains grounded
but keeps an eye on the sky

plants extra for birds to eat their fill
and never leaves us hungry

—MARY KOLADA SCOTT

A GARDENER'S PRAYER

When I rise
let me plant
the sweet silence
of my garden as a seed
inside me, blooming
hour by hour, chasing away
the weeds of the day
until I retire
and the sweet silence
sings my soul to sleep
once again.

—ARLENE GAY LEVINE

three

GARDENING

Gardening is any way that humans and nature come together with the intent of creating beauty.

—TINA JAMES

REFLECTIONS ON GARDENING

Connection with gardens, even small ones, even potted plants, can become windows to the inner life. The simple act of stopping and looking at the beauty around us can be prayer.

—PATRICIA R. BARRETT

I have never had so many good ideas day after day as when I worked in the garden.

—JOHN ERSKINE

Successful gardening is doing what has to be done when it has to be done the way it ought to be done whether you want to do it or not.

—JERRY BAKER

It seemed to my friend that the creation of a landscape-garden offered to the proper muse the most magnificent of opportunities. Here indeed was the fairest field for the display of the imagination, in the endless combining of forms of novel beauty.

—EDGAR ALLAN POE (1809–1849)

Working in the garden gives me something beyond the enjoyment of the senses. It gives me a profound feeling of inner peace.

—RUTH STOUT (1884–1980)

There can be no other occupation like gardening in which, if you were to creep up behind someone at their work, you would find them smiling.

—MIRABEL OSLER

Gardening is the art that uses flowers and plants as paint, and the soil and sky as canvas.

—ELIZABETH MURRAY

But each spring....a gardening instinct, sure as the sap rising in the trees, stirs within us. We look about and decide to tame another little bit of ground.

—LEWIS GANTT

Gardening is medicine that does not need a prescription...and with no limit on dosage.

—AUTHOR UNKNOWN

Gardening is the best therapy in the world. You can put so much into it and get so much back…. How lucky we are to live on this beautiful earth—you can bring the beauty to yourselves through gardening.

—C. Z. GUEST (1920–2003)

OUR PERSONAL WORK OF ART

I have found, through years of practice, that people garden in order to make something grow; to interact with nature; to share, to find sanctuary, to heal, to honor the earth, to leave a mark. Through gardening, we feel whole as we make our personal work of art upon our land.

—JULIE MOIR MESSERVY

GROUND

For any number of ills
that assail the human heart,
loneliness, worry, gall,
boredom, anguish, greed—
touch dirt every day.

For whatever ails,
touch dirt every day.
Grab it in great handfuls.
Knead moistened clumps of clay.
Sift sand like streaming velvet.

Be cooled; be calmed.
Feel comfort in its smudge.
For whatever ails
and is grievous to your heart,
touch dirt every day.

—MARYANNE HANNAN

AUGUST CLEARING

Like a beautiful woman in need of a haircut,
her garden shouts evidence of her discontent.
Weeds reach hip-deep, seed pods
need dead-heading. Leaves wither,
brown and crackly below late blooming phlox.

Unable to bear it, she ignores tools at her side,
tears at weeds bare handed.
Soil crumbles, dark and rich under her fingers.
Bees take flight at her approach.
White butterfly balances on a wild aster,
unaware of her intentions
until she yanks the dried plant up by its roots,
shakes soil off, flings it aside.

At the end of the garden she turns,
draws a deep breath, surveys the damage.
Brown-eyed golden rudbeckia thriving,
dainty blue borage succulent in late summer heat,
yellow coreopsis neon bright
in its second bloom, stretches along the wall.

Knees buckle. She drops down
to sit on the cobblestone wall,
runs a roughened hand through damp hair.
Pressing both hands to her lower back,
she stretches, smiles, and feels
just a tiny bit better about herself.

—BARBARA J. GLYNN

GARDENING CREDO

I believe in the smell of dirt,
in the redemption of freshly-turned earth
and the ordered grace of furrows.
And, I believe in the industry of worms
whose unseen labor lets the soil
breathe easy—think yoga master.

I believe in the unpretentious turnip,
parsnip and potato with their quiet
underground life but also in rhubarb
which flaunts super-sized fans
above stately red stalks.

I admit I believe in weeds—horsetail,
purslane, creeping charlie—for back-
again persistence. And, I believe
that kneeling to tend a garden
is a hymn of humble praise.

—SUSAN J. ERICKSON

WHAT REMAINS

This year you'll start again
to loosen dirt and worms,
to toss one muddied worn rock
after another into the barrow
like the boy who skimmed stones on Lake Archer.
When the loam is smooth and supple,
you'll raise up the mounds;
each seed fingered from your pocket,
concealed by earth.

You've buried friends,
passed away like casings
taken by the wind,
but there's something in the weeding,
the hot ache of sun.
Some kind of consolation turned
abundant under your hoe.

—NANCY TUPPER LING

OLD GARDENER'S CONFESSION

How we ache for what we love:

     Cold and wet, we turn March soil
     Until stretched shoulders throb and burn.
     Plot by plot, we pull, unearth, and separate
     While joints and tendons swell in protest.
     Over beds of vegetables and flowers, we hover,
     Trowel or rake in hand, forgetful of the hours,
     Surprised our backs will not unbend upon command.

In the heat of August, callused and sun-beaten,

     We grapple weeds, untangle hoses, commiserate
     Across our lawns and hedges: we are tired, tired, tired
     Of the work that never ends: bring on the snow!
     We declare that we are ready for December,
     For peaceful and unbroken hours, feet up and
     Backs reclined, in our fireside chairs.

And yet

     Long before each winter's end,
     Before the last gray snowdrift disappears,
     Before Earth's straw and ochre palette returns,
     Our old hearts ache again—
     Ache for any hope of color:

The smallest hint of chartreuse-green
Waving from the willow,
A dot or two of yellow crocus,
A brave blue scilla star.

At each simple sign,
Something deep within us warms and stirs,
Watches and waits,
Until bud by bud, blade by blade,
Renewed by love, unmindful of pain,
We are born again.

—DIANNE M. DEL GIORNO

GARDENER'S WINTER LAMENT

Odds and ends of clean-up chores
put off till today. Now in rubber boots
digging hole for pot-bound cypress.

Drooping Mexican heather, soft
purple fuzz, must wait. Shears need
sharpening. Mist turns to rain.

Retreat indoors, dry hair, wipe mud
off dog's feet, put kettle on.
Can't ever keep up with nature.

Wrap chilled fingers around mug—
grateful my garden always needs me.

—ARLENE L. MANDELL

A GARDENER'S SPRINGTIME PRAYER

Here are my hands, Spirit of Earth and Space,
mysterious Wisdom within and behind everything that is
and is promising,

Gardener ever ancient, ever new,
who fashioned out of those colossal explosions at our beginning
all the avenues to life, to its complexities,
and to the communion we are destined for,
here are my hands.

Give them the skills of a midwife
to put good order into expectations,
to coax along the natural forces of life and growth
that are already within the earth,
and to help wisely with the harvesting.

Here are my hands,
and here are my dreams.

—WILLIAM CLEARY (1926–2012)

SPRING RAKING

After the long winter, the sun streaming down on a warm April day is a welcome blessing. Raking away the dried leaves and beige-brown strands of dead grass to give the new growth below a chance to thrive feels less like a tedious chore, and more like helping out with God's work. Not that God needs the help. More as if, like a benevolent parent, God has provided this as an opportunity to feel useful, like one is contributing.

And as I rake, I reflect that gardening is like that. We can tend the seed, provide adequate water, plant in the right place, and pull the weeds, but it is some power beyond ours that draws forth flowers and fruit, and causes the green things to grow and the colors to change in the fall.

Gardening is a kind of partnership with God. By holding up our end of it, we can make the final product better. But without the other partner, our efforts would be meaningless, for the wonders and miracles of nature require a power far deeper and more compelling than our own.

But these thoughts are too deep for an April day. Surrounded by birdsong and the earthy smell of green things coming back to life, it is enough to be outdoors, forget about the frustrations of work and daily life, and simply strive to be one with the rake and the grass and the fresh air. And on an early spring day, this is blessing enough.

—LISA TIMPF

GARDEN GIFT

Weary, dispirited,
I unlatch the garden gate

see scarlet roses scaling the trellis,
touch fronds of stretching fern,
stop to *taste* tender leaves of thyme.

Gathering an armful of lilacs,
I bury my head in the fragrance.

Again, I stop. This time to *listen.*
The resident robin is serenading
his mate.

I close the gate,
jauntily carry my bouquet.

—DEMAR REGIER

SPIRITUAL GARDENING

Gardening is never simply about gardens. It is work that reveals the meaning and character of humanity, and is an exercise and demonstration of who we take ourselves and creation to be. It is the most direct and practical site where we can learn the art and discipline of being creatures. Here we concretely and practically see how we relate to the natural world, to other creatures, and ultimately to the Creator. We discover whether we are prepared to honor these relations by nurture and care and celebration, or despise and abuse them. Gardens are a microcosm of the universe in which all the living and nonliving elements of life meet, elements ranging from geological formations and countless biochemical reactions to human inventiveness and age-old traditions about cuisine and beauty. When and how we garden gives expression to how we think we fit in the world. Through the many ways we produce and consume food, we bear witness to our ability or failure to gratefully and humbly receive creation as a gift from God.

To garden effectively is to bring human living into fairly close, appreciative, and sympathetic alignment with the life going on in the garden. It requires us to know a particular plot of land and understand its potential, and then work harmoniously with it. To garden is to unseat oneself as the center of primary importance, and to instead turn one's life into various forms of service that will strengthen and maintain the many memberships that make up the garden....

Gardening, besides being a practical, life-nurturing task, is also always a spiritual activity. In it people attempt to make visible and tasty what is good, beautiful, and even holy. Every act of gardening presupposes and embodies a way of relating to creation, a way that invariably invokes moral and spiritual decisions.... Our aim must be to develop into good gardeners, gardeners who work harmoniously among the flows of life. This means that besides vegetables, flowers, and fruit, gardeners are themselves undergoing a spiritual cultivation into something beautiful and sympathetic and healthy. A caring, faithful, and worshipping humanity is one of the garden's most important crops.

—NORMAN WIRZBA

YOUR FLOWERS ARE PRETTY

body bent
by too many years

propped up with a silver cane
feet doing a slow shuffle

he wobbles along holding a green bucket
totters over every flower
scoops each a dipper of water

he moves

from geranium
to geranium
to geranium

like a honey bee
floating
across the white porch
of the Sunnyside Retirement Center

he makes them bloom
they keep him
moving

—SHERYL L. NELMS

GARDEN CONFESSIONAL

My hands nestle into loam
Bare and eager for earth's communion.
If this be my penance, then no sin
Can not be cleansed by dirt.
The till, the hoe, the sweet smell of soil
Make hale and merry. At day's end
They take my humble confession
And forgive me my daily toils.
Lead me not into temptation
But into this garden chapel
With pews of lettuce, carrot, and sweet pea.
My knees bent in reverence,
The altar all around.

—JILL MCCABE JOHNSON

four

THE SEASONS

If winter comes, can spring be far behind?

—PERCY BYSSHE SHELLEY (1792–1822)

TO EVERYTHING THERE IS A SEASON

To everything there is a season,

a time for every purpose under the sun:

A time to be born and a time to die;

a time to plant and a time to pluck up that which is planted.

—ECCLESIASTES 3:1–2

PSALM OF PRAISE

Sing for joy in summer
When earth is bright and green.
Sing with fun in winter
When snow is velveteen.
In spring sing out with gusto
For the life to soon unfold—
And sing with zest in autumn
For the woodlands colored gold.

—JOAN STEPHEN

TREES

In spring the trees reach into heaven,
Their green leaves leap into the sky,
In summer they are gentle friends
That seem to smile as the winds sigh—
In autumn they turn every garden
Into a golden mystery,
But winter is their time for prayer,
In silent, snowy worlds a tree
Becomes an artist's dream to paint,
As it stands lowly in the sod,
Our hearts like poets see the trees
Arrows that point the way to God.

—MARION SCHOEBERLEIN

SUDDENLY,

it's almost spring, and the new blue sky
is full of clouds, blowing and tossing
like somebody's wash, even though the air's
still cold and the ground's still hard. If you look
hard, you can see buds starting to swell, stick
their little chests out, and look, here are the first
stabs at green, crocus and daffodils piercing their way
through dirt's dark cloth. Even though finches are still wearing
their winter coats, those dull serviceable tweeds,
the fields on the tawny hills have shifted into green,
full speed ahead, and robins have set their alarm clocks
and are up early, catching the etc.
Everywhere, bare branches toss in the wind, hello, hello, hello.

—BARBARA CROOKER

SPRING PLEDGE

I pledge allegiance to the flag,
graceful sword-leaved iris,
boldly veined with down curved sepals.
I pledge allegiance to wild hyacinth
with keeled leaves, six pointed stars.
I pledge pickerel weed
whose blue spires edge pond and stream.
I pledge blue and purple,
the united states of spring.
And to the republic of painted trillium
whose crimson blazes
at the base of white petals.
One meadow, one woodland
under God, indivisible
with violet and larkspur for all!

—SHIRLEY S. STEVENS

SNOWFLAKES OF SPRING

Our street is adrift with flowering pear.
A blizzard of petals whirls through the air,
As clouds cover gently each gnarly black limb,
Then cascade to earth at the merriest whim.
Gutters and sidewalks and rose bushes all
Disappear 'neath the white of this silent snowfall
As completely as any harsh winter can bring.
But, oh, what a wonder, these snowflakes of spring!

—BONNIE COMPTON HANSON

THIS SUMMER DAY

That sprinkler is at it again,
        hissing and spitting its arc
of silver, and the parched
        lawn is tickled green. The air
hums with the busy traffic
of butterflies and bees,
who navigate without lane
        markers, stop signs, directional
signals. One of my friends
        says we're now in the shady
side of the garden, having moved
past pollination, fruition,
and all that bee-buzzed jazz,
into our autumn days. But I say wait.
It's still summer, and the breeze is full
of sweetness spilled from a million
petals; it wraps around your arms,
lifts the hair from the back of your neck.
The salvia, coreopsis, roses
have set the borders on fire,
and the peaches waiting to be picked
are heavy with juice. We are still ripening
into our bodies, still in the act of becoming.

Rejoice in the day's long sugar.
Praise that big fat tomato of a sun.

—BARBARA CROOKER

AND WHAT IS SO RARE
AS A DAY IN JUNE?

And what is so rare as a day in June?
    Then, if ever, come perfect days;
Then Heaven tries the earth if it be in tune,
    And over it softly her warm ear lays:
Whether we look, or whether we listen,
We hear life murmur, or see it glisten;
Every clod feels a stir of might,
    An instinct within it that reaches and towers,
And, grasping blindly above it for light,
    Climbs to a soul in grass and flowers….

—JAMES RUSSELL LOWELL (1819–1891)

DIMINUENDO

Late August, and the fields are singing with insects,
goldenrod blessing the air.
The hillside springs with grasshoppers
drunk on the last dregs of sun.
Queen Anne's lacework is edging the path
where even the grasses are shining silver,
lifted, as in common prayer,
by the diminishing wind.
Out in the fields, the corn stands shock still;
the stalks have become the color of air.
Their fingers point north, where the snow is waiting.
All of the apples have gathered in redness,
a thousand sunsets burn in the trees.
Soon, they will drop and split,
and the whirling wasps will leave only the cores,
the spaces that remain.

—BARBARA CROOKER

SUMMER PASSING

The soft silence of this
afternoon,
the light breeze, the
bright skies
suggest that summer will
soon pass;
and the world, clothed
in her somber
beauty, will again know
the glory that
time alone creates.
For time
continues her rush to
the past with
life ever drawn to
the new;
and we, each aware of
our journey
and flight, are awed
by the fast
passing view.

—THOMAS L. REID

LEAVES FALLING

look at them
pray to them
all the leaves
falling off a tree
watch them dance in the autumn wind
and paint the sky with fire

—MIKE BLOTTENBERGER

TO MARIGOLDS IN AUTUMN

I have watched your fiery dances in the sun,
your galaxy aflame beside my door;
but now that summer's gone and autumn's come,
I see your blazing symphony no more.

You were but small, dark specks within my hand
when spring disrobed and changed from white to green;
but in your darkness lay a golden plan;
and there was light, and what a light was seen!

So quickly have you come and quickly gone,
yet in your life a somber truth you give.
Our life and death are really only one;
we begin to die the hour we begin to live.

And since we too must pass and cease to live,
our blossom fading quickly in the sun,
we know it's not important what we have,
but what we are, what we do, what we become.

—THOMAS L. REID

ALL BECAUSE AUTUMN CAME

The Autumn wind rattles the trees
—I shiver just a little—
For it won't be long till Winter's winds
Make the branches brittle.

I pull my chair up to the fire
And watch the dancing flames,
Relishing warmth and coziness...
All because Autumn came.

Tomorrow we'll rake up the leaves
Into a great big pile,
And watch the kids as they jump in,
So happy all the while.

Then hot cocoa is in order
To chase the chill away,
And we'll sit around the table
To plan another day.

I'm so thankful for the seasons
And the changes they bring!
Each happy little pleasure can
Cause the heart to sing.

—DENISE A. DEWALD

LADY AUTUMN

Lady Autumn, richly garbed,
     dazzling and dignified,
     touched in briefest glimpse
     by the chill of coming winter.
Memories of summer warmth,
     golden rays, and fragrances
     of blossoms touched with dew
     are manifest in aging splendor.
Still, evenings early descend
     with crisp September breezes,
     changing green to red and umber,
     supple twigs to brittle branches.
Yet gracefully, the Lady stands,
     accepting times and seasons.
     In beautiful maturity...
     she trusts the Master Plan.

—EMILY KING

CONTRACTIONS

One more walk through my
backyard sanctuary
before snow blankets
the earth.

I will miss every finally realized rose.
I have known their sweet essence
more in recent days than ever before.

Gratefully I snip their boney branches
and insulate their tender roots
to bring them through as they have me.

A dense, dusky sadness
descends.

It takes so long.

—HAZEL SMITH HUTCHINSON

IT'S EARLY WINTER

It's early winter, and the begonias have delivered a second bloom.
Scarlet blossoms hang heavily from their brittle stems; peach-hued
blossoms as large as my head mingle with yellow ones, orange, apricot
and pink. The annual beds are still an embarrassing spectacle of
color—cyclamen, azaleas, even a lily has held off its bloom until now. I
step down the stone walk toward the house, absorbed in the dazzle of
the garden, and the hummingbird that hectored me all summer when
I watered, spins just inches before my face. I stumble on the brick walk,
and the small bird hovers over me for a long moment, its crimson head
chattering, then swings back to its home hidden deep in the ferns.

—GARY YOUNG

WINTER BLESSING

As the snow covers,
The ground stays moist and insulated,
Ready for the next season's sowing,
Growing, and harvest.
This is a time of preparation,
A time of stillness and quiet.
Even the creatures of the ground
Sleep in their dark, silent homes.
This is an ending, and a beginning,
An open season of plans and possibilities.
May this season of rest
Bring forth richness and beauty
In the months to come.

—PAULA E. KIRMAN

JANUARY THAW

False spring.
The sun, thinned
to a white radiance,
warms the bones,
pulses the thermometer up over sixty.
Crocuses push their tips
through the newly softened earth.
Too soon, we say,
and want to make them
retrieve their leaves,
refurl them back.
Shrink, before the snow returns,
or you won't live to dazzle us
with your watered silks
of purple, white, gold.
We haven't had a proper winter yet,
the ground still brown,
no real accumulations.
But in this fickle weather,
we warm, too,
turn our faces upward
to the light,
shed our coats, gloves, scarves.

Sheets of ice begin to fall away.
And suddenly, our skin is alive again.
Shyly, small flowers open in our hearts.

—BARBARA CROOKER

LATE FEBRUARY,

and light begins to soften
around the edges. Snow's flannel
sheets recede, fold back, and look,
the grass is still there,
a fresh green quilt waiting
to be hung on the line.
Crocus cut their teeth
in perennial beds.
Spring holds her breath.
White-throated sparrows
whistle up the sun.
Every day, another cup of light.

—BARBARA CROOKER

five

PLANTING & HARVESTING

Earth is here so kind, that just tickle her with a hoe and
she laughs with a harvest.

—DOUGLAS JERROLD (1803–1857)

THE PROMISE

A plot of earth
waits for me
to plant my seeds
before the sun.
The garden calls
to my heart,
as I play joyfully
in the soil,
dreaming of
their sweet flowering.

—JOAN NOËLDECHEN

LITURGY

every year
the annual rite
plow
plant
water
watch
wait
wonder
and harvest.
enduring
early snow
frozen ground
spring flood
summer drought.
weeds and seeds
birds and bugs.

—Me HANSBURG

TURNING THE GARDEN UNDER,

as the hoe whispers erase, erase,
and last year's neat rows disappear,
the final editing.
Unlike paper, the ground forgives,
eager to begin again, fill up with green.
The garden accepts whatever is sown:
scratch out carrots, they appear.
Imagine pumpkins, heavy and fat
as summer storms, and, surprised
as Cinderella, you find them in August.
Nothing is as clean as dirt.

—BARBARA CROOKER

THE GARDENER

Precious seed,
My Love has been in the tilling,
Tending,
And timely nurturing.
Growth, never guaranteed.

Precious flower,
My joy has been in the unfolding.
Your eyes, fully open now,
Go!
Show the world.

—MARY LENORE QUIGLEY

HARMONY

All that is harmony for thee, O Universe, is in harmony with me as well.
Nothing that comes at the right time for thee is too early or too late
for me. Everything is fruit to me that thy seasons bring, O Nature. All
things come of thee, have their being in thee, and return to thee.

—MARCUS AURELIUS (121–180 A.D.)

CHILD'S GARDEN BLESSING

Place carefully your seedling wishes
In these freshly tilled rows.
Sun, water and bashful prayers
Will nurture your hushed yet hopeful dreams.
Still-winged thrushes wait wide-eyed and breathless
On the promise of this harvest.
You don't need permission to flourish.
Success is your birthright.
Take liberties with our love.
Bloom big.

—JILL MCCABE JOHNSON

FOUR O'CLOCKS

Some flowers are pure magic. I first learned this when I got a packet
of flower seeds for a 4-H project one spring. The flowers were called
"Four O'clocks" and, as evidenced by the brightly colored picture on
the front, were quite showy. I eagerly dug up a bed in front of my house
and sowed the seeds in wobbly rows. Every day I ran out to check on
their progress which, of course, because I was an impatient eight-year-
old, wasn't quick enough for me.

Finally, after an agonizing couple of weeks the seedlings came
poking through. They grew pretty rapidly—those that could survive
my overwatering. (I must confess that I had gotten bored with the
plain green seedlings.) Then the first flower buds appeared. They all
burst into bloom on practically the same day, filling the front of my
house with a riot of color. I, too, was bursting with pride and made all
my family and neighbors look at the amazing miracle the seed packet
had produced. By the time I had rounded everybody up, however, the
flowers were closed up tightly. Every one of them! "That's why they're
called Four O'clocks," my mother explained. "Every day they close
up at four o'clock sharp and open up with the first ray of sun in the
morning."

I checked every day and she was right. Four o'clock sharp. You
could set your watch by the flowers!

—BRENDA KNIGHT

DISCOVERY

I bend down and release a small handful of seeds.
They settle on the soil below, tiny brown spots in an oasis of mud,
and I feel life's miracles just thinking
that a handful of water every day
will transform them, like a caterpillar to a butterfly.

I think of the first settlers and how they depended on these seeds,
lovingly caring for each plant,
knowing they would bring sustenance in the months ahead,
praying that the rains would come to bring them to fruition.
Their life was based on the land.
They knew every cycle of every season as they knew their own body.
I think of the settlers and I mourn at what we've lost.

The crops like magic mature into tall green plants,
full of round red fruit,
and I watch my granddaughter.
Just three years old, she's fascinated by this new life.
She picks a small, ripe tomato,
holds it in her hand, and her eyes grow wide with wonder.
She understands the miracle of life, the power of transformation.
She is connected to the land,
finding joy in the simple act of being…
and I rejoice as I realize we haven't lost it at all.

—BARB MAYER

MAKING SOUP FOR SELAH

...a poem for my granddaughter

I

All summer the sun and earth and rain
have nurtured this garden treasure,
and today, I pick it, peel it, chop, slice and dice
this golden butternut squash

then simmer it to softness with fennel, onion and garlic
until it becomes a magical birthday broth
into which I add a splash of oil, a pinch of ginger,
some salt and pepper and then

the final touches of buttermilk, yogurt,
and a dollop of sour cream.
Such rich pleasure it brings,
this pause to attend to you.

II

May this soup warm your savory spirit,
sustain you through the mystery
of each season's flow

may it enlarge the place where joy dances
in your heart, and may each spoonful nurture
the sweet harvest that has begun

the sweeter ones, still to come.

—MICHAEL S. GLASER

YOUR GIFT OF TOMATOES

You bring me the tight bloody suns of October
snatched from vines which hide green snakes
and black-and-gold garden spiders.

You present tomatoes fragrant as love
in a basket of wicker.

Tomatoes escape through your fingers
as if harvest moons crowning, burst
in your palms, redden our destiny's map.
Their blood burns the cuts in my hands.

I try to tame them under my knife—sugar,
basil, parsley and salt—offer them sweet
and spicy as love on a bed of our lettuce.

Their flesh lights our throats with their glow.

All winter the garden lies pungent and cold.
Tomatoes still loll, green and hard under the snow.

Then again the carmine moon bursts through the sky.

—ELISAVIETTA RITCHIE

HARVEST TIME

These are the days
of remembering
summer's sizzling heat,
the cornucopia
overflowing with
fresh corn,
juicy tomatoes,
crunchy peppers,
tender carrots.

As birds turn
toward their trajectory
south, we rein in
appetites, prepare
for pumpkin pie,
crisp, cool apples,
the piquancy
of cider.

—SUSAN LANDON

FALL BOUNTY

Ginger & nutmeg
And cinnamon as well
All mingled with apples
Right out of the dell
A pumpkin with frost
Right up to the vine
Blessings Abound
At—
Harvest time!

—MARY MAUDE DANIELS

six

FLOWERS

Earth laughs in flowers.

—RALPH WALDO EMERSON (1803–1882)

I WANDERED LONELY AS A CLOUD

I wandered lonely as a cloud
That floats on high o'er vales and hills,
When all at once I saw a crowd,
A host, of golden daffodils;
Beside the lake, beneath the trees,
Fluttering and dancing in the breeze
Continuous as the stars that shine
And twinkle on the milky way,
They stretched in never-ending line
Along the margin of a bay:
Then thousand saw I at a glance,
Tossing their heads in sprightly dance.

—WILLIAM WORDSWORTH (1770–1850)

EARLY DAFFODILS

Six yellow-frilled portals
arching on green stems
arranged in a circle.

Early daffodils from your
tiny garden, tended by your hand,
drooping now in a glass vase

on our table, awaiting your return,
The slant sun touches each bloom,
an annunciation—pleated shadows,

gold glowing faces. The light effect
lasts a moment, less—and only
if your eyes are ready. As with any grace.

—STEVEN RATINER

FLOWERING TREES

There's a red cardinal in the cherry tree,
its branches adrift in bits of lace;
he's singing his heart out, "Here, here, here
I am, look at me." It is the season
of flowering trees, an astonishment
of blooms from bark. Look at the weeping cherries,
their lilac cascades; the cerise ruffles
of the flowering crabs; the magnolias
in their ball gowns; the dogwoods clouded
in white chiffon. Look at these lime green ribbons,
silks from a magician's hands. Why, the air
is in blossom, and we are still in love.

—BARBARA CROOKER

NEVER LOSE AN OPPORTUNITY

Never lose an opportunity of seeing anything that is beautiful,
for beauty is God's handwriting—a wayside sacrament.
Welcome it in every fair face, in every fair sky, in every fair flower,
and thank God for it as a cup of blessing.

—RALPH WALDO EMERSON (1803–1882)

AN ISLAND GARDEN

(Excerpt)

When in these fresh mornings I go into my garden before any one
is awake, I go for the time being into perfect happiness. In this hour
divinely fresh and still, the fair face of every flower salutes me with
a silent joy that fills me with infinite content; each gives me its color,
its grace, its perfume, and enriches me with the consummation of
its beauty. All the cares, perplexities, and griefs of existence, all the
burdens of life slip from my shoulders and leave me with the heart of
a little child that asks nothing beyond its present moment of innocent
bliss. These myriad beaming faces turned to mine seem to look at
me with blessing eyes. I feel the personality of each flower, and I
find myself greeting them as if they were human. "Good-morning,
beloved friends! Are all things well with you? And are you tranquil and
bright? And are you happy and beautiful?" They stand in their peace
and purity and lift themselves to my adoring gaze as if they knew my
worship—so calm, so sweet, so delicately radiant, I lose myself in the
tranquillity of their happiness.

—CELIA THAXTER (1835–1894)

FLOWERS

Forsythia, yellow butterflies dancing in a web
and pink magnolia thick like lips on trees
whose limbs wave wands across the dawn.
Roses curl, closed eyes on the vine,
faint bluish-purple veins rippling their buds
while daisies and tulips flutter in breeze
prepared flight of ballerinas *en pointe*,
on the tips of their toes, a soul composed
for the sympathy of flowers, so human yet divine.
A bouquet is a banquet to pluck petals that float
in miniature pond within turquoise bowl
as a body weak from winter bends to unwind
dreaming on the promises of spring
and the whispersong of nature unconfined.

—ROCHELLE LYNN HOLT

THE WILDING

Gardens of blossom in splendor,
Colors arranged as sown,
But none with beauty so rare
As the flower that stands alone.

Columbine and Indian Pipe,
Lady's Slipper of pink and gold;
Untamed treasures of nature
Are a glory to behold.

Fragile pixie of the wood,
No bouquet meant to be;
Bewitching is your charm
As long as you are free.

You bloom and die in solitude
Beyond the touch of care.
Your shining was not wasted—
God surely put you there.

—C. DAVID HAY

MORNING GLORIES

Morning glories wrap their curly tendrils
delicately around the balcony's cedar posts.
Left to their own design, they would entangle
in a willy-nilly mass of choking green.

I conduct these eight musicians.
Each morning, and sometimes again
at dusk, I entwine their fragile green stalks
across the railing

No hint of flowers, white or blue,
yet appears. Just the same,
I practice faith and forbearance on their behalf.

—STEPHANIE B. SHAFRAN

MORNING GLORIES

First thing
summer mornings

I would come out
to the porch,
tiptoe down the steps,
pad barefoot
across the grass

stand behind the trellis
and look up to see
how many of her
morning glories
had opened.

They were so blue
and pure, beaded
with dew

as if miniature
gateways to the skies
had swayed open

allowing me
to ramble
into infinity.

—NORBERT KRAPF

A POET'S PRAYER

The view from my window is lilies
Swaying gently with elegant grace,
Adorned with the glitter of night rain,
Catching the sun in petals upraised.

For great is the beauty of lilies
Asking little be given their way,
But the sun and the soil and the raindrops
And the peace of a warm summer's day.

So this is the gift of the lilies
Which arise every morn with the sun.
Though brief is their bloom and their color,
Their beauty forever goes on.

Lord, please let me be like the lilies,
Finding joy in the simplest of things
To fashion such beauty as lilies
With words that will make the heart sing.

—SANDRA E. MCBRIDE

LILIES

After the storm—
yellow lilies.
There you stand
holding a huge bouquet.
Mustard streaked petals
open
reaching back
wings flung wide.
Trumpeting courage
blowing jazzy joy.

—MEG CAMPBELL

I KNOW A BANK WHEREON
THE WILD THYME GROWS

I know a bank whereon the wild thyme blows,
Where oxlips and the nodding violet grows
Quite over-canopied with luscious woodbine,
With sweet musk-roses, and with eglantine:
There sleeps Titania some time of the night,
Lulled in these flowers with dances and delight.

—WILLIAM SHAKESPEARE (1564–1616)

THESE ROSES UNDER MY WINDOW

These roses under my window make no reference to former roses or to better ones; they are for what they are; they exist with God to-day. There is no time to them. There is simply the rose; it is perfect in every moment of its existence.

—RALPH WALDO EMERSON (1803–1882)

THE ROSE

Sitting peacefully
On her tall green stem
She sings her fragrance of love.
She opens easily,
Blossoming...
She trusts.
She is honest,
She is free.
Secure in her existence.
She simply is.
Her pink petals whisper to me.
She is my teacher.
She has much to give,
I have much to learn...

—FANNY LEVIN

MY NEIGHBOR'S ROSES

The roses red upon my neighbor's vine
Are owned by him, but they are also mine.
His was the cost, and his the labor, too,
But mine as well as his the joy, their loveliness to view.

They bloom for me and are for me as fair
As for the man who gives them all his care.
Thus I am rich because a good man grew
A rose-clad vine for all his neighbors' view.

I know from this that others plant for me,
And what they own my joy may also be;
So why be selfish when so much that's fine
Is grown for you upon your neighbor's vine?

—A. L. GRUBER

And here is

MY NEIGHBOR'S REPLY

Your neighbor, sir, whose roses you admire,
Is glad indeed to know that they inspire
Within your breast a feeling quite as fine
As felt by him who owns and tends that vine.

That those fair flowers should give my neighbors joy
But swells my own, and draws there from alloy
Which would lessen its full worth, did I not know
That others' pleasure in the flowers grow.

Friend, from my neighbors and this vine I've learned
That sharing pleasure means a profit turned;
And he who shares the joy in what he's grown
Spreads joy abroad and doubles all his own.

—AUTHOR UNKNOWN

THEIR GARDEN

She selects their flowers for delicacy of shape,
an elegant thrust of stamen or a pensive
droop of petal, their color and endurance,
a propensity to flourish in sunlight or shade,
while he chooses their names,
an excuse to say them all summer—
Hepatica and *periwinkle,* four lilting syllables
that trip off the tongue like children giggling
off a haystack. *Bachelor buttons*, shy, reliable.
Queen Anne's lace—aristocratic refinement
defying the culverts and canal sides where it thrives.
Black-eyed-Susans connoting robust, buxom
girls who will always have the chores done
and a good meal on the table.
And one that makes you wake
and ask the summer for its story,
the creeping-steadily-up-the-garden-trellis
morning glory.

—MAUREEN TOLMAN FLANNERY

AND THEY SAY THERE ARE NO MORE

The amaryllis blooms
effortlessly as we watch,
pale green stalk already extended
from the thick rough bulb.
Delicate greenery unfurls itself
like a translucent fan parting
to reveal wrinkled magenta velvet,
dark-veined and curling upward
as if in petal/prayer.
We worship
the slow-motion
birth
unfolding
as any true miracle.

—NITA PENFOLD

LOVELY CAMELLIA

You've been waiting
to blossom, lovely Camellia,
for a year—through summer,
fall and winter you waited—
buds locked tight—
for spring.

Now look at you!
Each petal gazing up
radiates soft pink,
veined with coral streams
that spread to the delta
from some unseen source:
In your heart, amid tiny pink ruffles,
dozens of uncrumpled golden-
tipped stamen offer themselves
to the birds and the honeybees.

No one has ever looked
like you before, or ever will again.
Your beauty comes straight
from Her Holiness,
the Queen of Life.

—JANINE CANAN

seven

FRUITS & VEGETABLES

The act of putting into your mouth what the earth has grown
is perhaps your most direct interaction with the earth.

—FRANCES MOORE LAPPÉ

SQUASH BLOSSOM

I am sitting in the sunny green, still damp
from a week of rain, near these happy yellow
children shaded by their flat green parents,
reminding me of the joy of growing things.

We start out closed like this, our baby hands
clenched and tense, reaching for that prehensile
branch. And then we begin to open. My daughter,
at twelve, is like this. Six petals reaching up

to the sun, with a fragile faint line down the
center of each one. Later we wilt, give way
to fruit, turn brown and surrender to being
undone. On fuzzy stalks from the mouth

of faded flowers, each new gourd will come.
All we need to know of love and sex and faith
and regeneration is in a squash blossom. I am
ready for communion. I tug and pick one.

—CASSIE PREMO STEELE

GARDEN

Sunlights in my garden stray and stumble
Down the paths, beside the plots where water
Drips and dribbles. As my cultivator
Chops and channels, so my plants assemble
In their vegetable splendor, their shows
Of shapes and shades and colors, textures strange
As any organs mammal boast. They range
Diverse, divulge their difference. Here grows
A jagged artichoke. There smooth green scale,
Asparagus. And lay the rich red rib
Of rhubarb underneath a poison bib.
See a carrot man in his earth jail
And sweet slick melon on his slip. I seed
The backyard soil and bring it to solution.
I bring my private order to confusion
And separate the greens to plant and weed.
A carnival extravaganza grows
In urban earth caged in my garden rows.

—LAURENCE SNYDAL

KINDNESS

A friendly kiss of kindness,
strawberries wear their seeds on their skin,
hearts on their sleeves,
tip their little green caps to passersby,
stems reaching out to form
compassionate handles and offer
a sympathetic sharing.

—SALLY CLARK

CHOKING

The neighbor's artichokes peek
over the fence, spiny verdigris heads
thatched with lilac hair.
They smolder like grenades,
send vague threats
across the redwood slats.
I thought artichokes
grew like melons—armadillos
snuffling against the earth—
but these pink buds
are air born, wavering
high and top heavy
on their tendony stalks,
daring me to lop off their heads,
dance them onto a plate,
tear off their stiff veils
one by dusky one until I find
the damp vegetable fur,
the fibrous button,
the bitter and buttery heart.

—GAYLE BRANDEIS

TOMATO

It is not the tomatoes, really,
nor the seed weight that fills their skins

that solid but
tenuous heft;

nor the kernel of light
you feel hidden in the pit of each.

Something there is just south of a word,
regarding the radiant wedges that slip
from the knife
to the damp cutting board,

that sends us back out
to the garden.
We groom the soft leaves,
passing sacks to the basket,

red tumbled on red till the heart swims with it.
Our well-loaded wicker was worth the new trip.

In the kitchen the dish-rattling feels like comfort,
the routine meal
        is a blessed thing:

astonishing to eat,
graced by such company,
our muted mouths gleaming with prayer.

—WILLIAM OREM

HOLY TOMATOES

I pluck tomatoes from the vines,
feel them sun-warmed and firm in my hands.
Such gifts arriving in our daily dirt.

Light pours through the window
as I rinse them in the sink.
Water droplets shimmer,
poised on skins red as love.

I am held here, like the dust motes
floating in a beam of light,
caught in that sunstream.

How the world offers itself up.
Sunlight spills through the window
and the tomatoes glow, opulent spheres
each one round, full, complete.

—GINNY LOWE CONNORS

RASPBERRIES

Fall crop:
juicy druples,
carmine thimbles,
little beehives, ruddy nipples
dangle from the arching branches,
fall lightly into our cupped hands.
Just a touch uncouples
these plump droplets
from their cores.
The centers are hollow,
our tongues just fit;
crushed in our mouths,
the berries turn to wine;
even the bees
are drunk on this redness.
O September!
When the rest of the garden
dwindles to meager,
when the trees begin
their strip to the bones,
you come to fruit
bearing rubies on your canes,
and we're on our knees,
stained in crimson,
our garnet fingers
praising the earth.

—BARBARA CROOKER

SHELLING PEAS

for my mother

We're shelling peas, gently rocking on the swing
that hangs on chains from the roof of the porch
at my grandparents' house.

I'm four years old, wedged between Mother and Nana,
Singing as we swing, I balance a metal pot on my knees
as peas rattle into it from their nimble hands.

Newly picked from the garden out back, the pods are still
warm from the sun. I take pleasure in the sudden give
along each seam, the stream of peas into my waiting palm.

Now and then I eat a handful, sweet-bitter on my tongue,
savoring their rawness, the scent of earth, the mystery
of taste revealed as I crunch their hard round bodies.

Feet not touching the floor, eyes even with the lattice-work
under the porch railing, I sway and dream in the shifting
light and shade of a long summer afternoon.

The owl and the pussycat went to sea / in a beautiful pea-green boat,

my mother recites to me at bedtime, her weight on the side of
    my bed,
her voice almost chanting this poem she has loved since childhood.

A blessing in my mouth, those pale, hard peas, which I taste
even now as I chew on this memory, hungry for a pea-green boat
I might go out to sea in, trawling for light among the watery stars.

—PENNY HARTER

AVOCADO

Sylvia Plath wrote a poem
where she likens pears
to buddhas, how they ripen
like fat buddhas on the tree.
This was my avocado,
fat little Buddha
in my back yard, beaming
at me from its leafy branch
until I brought it inside
where it now sits zazen
in the wire basket
over the sink,
waiting for the moment
of enlightenment,
endarkenment,
its dark skin wrinkled
as an elephant, never forgetting
its own moist flesh,
never forgetting
its slippery, soapy, seed,
waiting for a finger
to press into its belly
so it can yield,

yield, yield
like bread dough,
like sand at the lip
of the sea,
for when a knife parts
its pachydermic skin,
it yields with all its heart,
a Buddha letting go
of attachment,
releasing its sage-
leaf fragrance
into the air,
releasing its life
like butter
on my tongue.

—GAYLE BRANDEIS

ORCHARD BLESSING

Even if I knew that tomorrow the world would go to pieces,
I would still plant my apple tree.

—MARTIN LUTHER

Apple round and red,
Bestow upon my dear one's head
These many blessings:

A trunk firm enough to found tree houses,
Hold cats and squirrels,
Withstand the axe;

Branches supple as giant arms
Strong enough to carry singing birds,
Laughing children in swings;

Leaves a green tent against sun or rain;
In fall, the wild and calling scent
Of gold adventure;

Sweet flowers that hum white promise
To the bees and me, a tune
That causes even Spring to swoon;

Fruit generous, sweet or crisp or sour,
Each bearing stars, the seeds of a future
Kind as all of the above.

Like love.

—MARJORIE ROMMEL

PEAR TREE AT SUNSET

I am waiting for little nuggets of pear
to appear where blossoms first succumbed to bees
and their sexy buzz deep into the center of all possible.

I am waiting for the sun's last angle of gold
to pour into the pear's heart and hum there
like bees did in their sticky passion

so that when I bite into the plump body of pear
strands of light and the sweet buzz of late afternoon
will sing from my mouth into yours when we kiss.

—LISA ZIMMERMAN

eight

ALL CREATURES

To me, the garden is a doorway to other worlds;
one of them, of course, is the world of birds.

—ANNE RAVER

LEAP FROG

you jump
up over the spires
of red hollyhocks

sail through the blue
delphinium

plop into the
lily of the valley
perfume

nestle down
in the moss
beside
the back porch

do your short hop
under the
trellis

of American Beauties
raining their faded
petals into
your pond

where you settle in mud

until a sudden shatter
by the wind
sends you

leap frogging again.

—SHERYL L. NELMS

WARTS

In a good perennial garden you
shouldn't see dirt; flowers
should be close, but not touching.
There should be harmony of color,
shape, and season—pale pink peony
next to violet iris and in front,
airy stalks of lavender.

I pull away the ferny branches
of Sweet Cicely to douse the
cracked hard clay the drought's
made; a dusty clod blinks at me,
darkens under trickling water,
stretches small appendages, almost
toes, in the new mud as if he were
almost smiling. I let the fronds
fall back. Even if we're close,
we shouldn't touch.

—HELEN RUGGIERI

BUMBLE BEES IN BLOOM

May flowers bring the bumble bees,
weeding, I kneel in their garden—
partaking from the communion table of Spring.

Like a humble peasant
I watch
among hovering, royal gardeners.

I gaze over fields of wild dandelion—
in trance
worshipping the bees
in their busy, buzzing
nectar-dance.

—JILL MORGAN CLARK

CYCLE: FOR THE DEER

Let them take both plantings of tender beans,
    The peppers which had started to bloom,
        The tomato vines with their blusters of small green fruit.
Let them nip in the bud every bellflower and chrysanthemum,
    The vibrant plantings of dianthus and petunias,
        The succulent patches of impatiens and portulaca.
Let the does—
    My night-browsing garden thieves—
        Be round and nourished going into the winter.
So when summer spins again,
    They will bring shy-eyed,
        Spindly-legged,
           White-dappled babies,
Who will soon prance spritely in their mothers' footsteps
        And take both plantings of tender beans...

—SHARON HUDNELL

BLESSINGS

The red butterflies
pause like blossoms
on the grass;
a yellow sunset
turns them bronze.
I am counting
pairs of red wings.
The late light
lies prayer-like,
slant and serene,
and I know
blessings
have lives of their own,
are surprising, can
suddenly
settle, or
fly away.

—BARBARA J. VAN NOORD

THE BUTTERFLY BALLET

Dancing over the garden
In their orange shoes,
Laughing on the grasses,
Playing on the dews,
Stealing sunbeam kisses,
Running in the rain,
Flying black-jeweled flowers
In a country lane,
Colors of the rainbow
In your pretty wings,
Ballet of the butterflies
When the summer sings.

—MARION SCHOEBERLEIN

IN THE GARDEN WITH MY GRANDSON

On this hot humid Iowa summer day,
we water seven clay pots of flowers,
pick off the spent geraniums,

mist the basil, pull meddlesome weeds,
check the ripening cherry tomatoes.
He fills the bird feeder to the brim

with safflower and thistle seed.
Taking up his own perch, he watches
quietly and detects birds that are rarely here:

the purple finch, downy woodpecker,
warbler, waxwing, golden crowned kinglet.
In hospitality, he fills the birdbath

with cool clean water overflowing.
Witnessing his vigilance and care,
I too, am filled to the brim, overflowing.

—DONNA WAHLERT

A HUMMINGBIRD MOMENT

To witness a two-inch miracle
Beating air at an invisible rate
Be alert in the slice of seconds
It takes for nectar to satiate

To see flickering iridescence
Vibrating gossamer wings
Be still, observe with wonder
The precision that hovering brings

To view a midair refueling
Of nature's tiniest aircraft
Be in awe, or you'll surely miss
The dart of her vibrant updraft.

—GWYNETH M. BLEDSOE

THE VISIT

It was a seasonal ritual.
Each fall my mother
filled the red feeder
and hung it by her
bedroom window
hoping to glimpse
a hummingbird.
But none came...
until my father died.
The next day
a ruby-throated, iridescent beauty
appeared, sipped, hovered, lingered.
It's a sign, I whispered,
that he's among us still.
Later, I recanted.
Silly girl to think
a soul would come
in the guise of a bird.
Yet, every October,
I hang the feeder
by my window
and wait.

—ANN REISFELD BOUTTÉ

MY GARDEN'S PROTECTED

My garden's protected
Have no fear
Not a creature is stirring
Not a sound do you hear

They work as a tag team
By day, and by night
Keeping critters away
Chase them off, with a fright.

No mouses, no birdies
We'll have none of those
No squirrelies or possums
And no need for scarecrows

My garden's protected
By better than that
My garden's protected
By my two scaredy cats.

—ROBIN M. SVEDI

KATYDID

Who rubbed its wings
like an angel's, pale green?

Katydid.

Who warned us all
of the coming fall?

Katydid.

Who made a chorus
of cricket noise for us?

Katydid.

Who saw lime wings
on grasshoppers that sing?

Katy did.

Who heard their song
and went chirping along?

Katy did.
Katydid.

—MAUREEN TOLMAN FLANNERY

CRICKET'S CODA

enjoy this day
for with the night frost
the crickets will die—

their song,
our constant companion
and summertime theme,
has but a few more measures to play—

and in the quiet of tomorrow,
when their faithful chorus
has been coldly rewarded,
let us mourn their passing.

—REBECCA K. WYSS

BURIED TREASURE

'Round and 'round the yard he runs
Autumn's little pirate
busy hunting in the dirt
to find his winter diet
fuzzy chestnuts, bulbs, and nuts
he scampers to and fro
looking for his buried treasure
before the falling snow
his bushy tail is twitching
as he sits up straight and tall
if only he remembered
where he hid them all.

—NANCY LYNCH GIBSON

THE GARDEN WARBLER

In spring they return to my garden
to build their nests,
to sing their songs.

But how do these tiny birds,
flying all the way from Africa,
know how to find my dwelling
in a crowded city?

It is a mystery.

Perhaps they follow the stars.
Perhaps their memories, sharper than mine,
bring them back to a friendly place in the sun
like a compass brings a sailor home.

Perhaps...

But such questions suddenly seem unimportant in April
when the Garden Warblers arrive in my backyard,
ready for hard work,
ready to fill the air with their songs.

Whatever magic or science
brings them here,

I am happy for their company.

—RAMNATH SUBRAMANIAN

A GARDENER'S LAMENT

It's summer now, and once again,
The battle, it is on,
To reap the harvest from the plants
Of all the seeds I've sown.

One would think with all my work,
And tender, loving care
A garden bounty I would reap,
But no, they do not share!

I refer to all the creatures
Who dine on the buffet
Provided by my garden
On any summer day.

Green beetles eat my zinnias.
The groundhogs eat my corn.
The squirrels and deer eat everything.
I often feel forlorn.

The birds dine on my berries,
The cut worms eat the vine
Of squash and watermelons,
And tomatoes quite divine.

The rabbits eat my parsley.
The chipmunks eat the seeds.
Can someone, please, explain to me
Why none of them eat weeds?

—SUSANNE WIGGINS BUNCH

MAKING THE ROUNDS

There's lots of the
Same old same old going on
This tasty blue morning

As the redbib quickzips
Sticks its pollinated nose
Into the business of tiger lilies

First it sweeps in and kisses
The pumpkin orange buds
Of the sugar sweet flower

Then climbs to the drooping petals
Of the shady hosta hiding in shadows
Scoots to the butterfly bush's sweet scones

As an encore the hummer
Quickflys and dances updown
Darts back and forth for seconds
Then zips off on another flashflitting flight

—GARY E. MCCORMICK

BIRDS AT THE FEEDER

A stream of chickadees arrive in a black and white blur at the maple tree feeder. The first bird grabs a safflower seed in his beak, then flits away to a small twig of the tree to eat it. The others, lined up like Montessori children, take their turns—seeds in bill, twigs bouncing under their soft landings. When the last in line has plucked his kernel, the first chickadee returns for a second helping. This courteous buffet line continues.

The male cardinal, with huffed red chest, fetches a sunflower seed for his orange-breasted mate. He feeds her—beak to beak, eye to eye. Only then does he return for his own morsel. The couple feeds; they sing their songs to one another.

A hefty pair of mourning doves plop on the tray of the feeder—too large to straddle the tiny metal prongs. In languor, they dine on the grains dropped in haste by the chickadees. They scud away and perch on the crossbar of a swingset where they nuzzle and preen, groom the Quaker-gray feathers of the other like an old married couple.

The birds shame me! It is only after I pause and watch them at the feeder that I remember the songs I want to sing to you.

—DONNA WAHLERT

HONORED BEES

In my garden, the roses have never been bigger—
coral, crimson, pink and yellow!
Ruby hummingbirds buzz at the feeder.

Birds chirp, sparrows splash, black bumbles
savor wisteria's tumbling purple.
A golden wasp shoots from the fragrant bouquet.

Everywhere fruit and vegetables
are waiting for pollen. Oh Bees,
thank you for visiting my happy garden!

—JANINE CANAN

nine

REFLECTIONS

Always remember the beauty of the
garden, for there is peace.

—AUTHOR UNKNOWN

REFLECTIONS

I like trees because they seem more resigned to the way they have to live than other things do.

—WILLA CATHER (1873–1947)

Knowing trees, I understand the meaning of patience.
Knowing grass, I can appreciate persistence.

—HAL BORLAND

No occupation is so delightful to me as the culture of the earth, and no culture comparable to that of the garden...
But though an old man, I am but a young gardener.

—THOMAS JEFFERSON (1743–1826)

I plant the seed,
You make it grow.
You send the rain,
I work the hoe.

—AUTHOR UNKNOWN

I'd rather have roses on my table than diamonds on my neck.

—EMMA GOLDMAN (1869–1940)

Of all the gifts I have each year
(Some sparkling bright and glowing)
I think the gifts I hold most dear,
Are the ones so green and growing.

—AUTHOR UNKNOWN

TO BE OF THE EARTH

To be of the Earth is to know
the restlessness of being a seed
the darkness of being planted
the struggle toward the light
the pain of growth into the light
the joy of bursting and bearing fruit
the love of being food for someone
the scattering of your seeds
the decay of the seasons
the mystery of death and
the miracle of birth.

—JOHN SOOS

THE GARDEN

Whenever I am troubled,
With a burden on my chest,
I hurry to the garden,
A spot that I love best.
Down on my knees, I close my eyes
And lift my arms up high.
Release a torrent weight of pain
Beneath a clear blue sky.
A cool, fresh breeze surrounds me
It soothes my troubled heart.
And I know that God is here
And had been from the start.
The proof is all around me
As I look upon the sod,
A harvest of life protruding
Indeed a gift from God.

—TEREASA BELLEW

CURATOR

In the coolness of the morning, the flowers are in full smiles,
heavenly blue morning glories dance upon their vines.
Peach colored gladiolas stand tall and beautiful,
holding hands with the pink and yellow hollyhocks beside them.
Yellow finches torpedo dive into the multi-hued sunflowers.
I am the first generation to make my living away from the farm,
but it has come with me, and I feel like a curator in a garden museum.
My city neighbors stop and ask, "What is that growing there?"
I remember the planning, the planting, and the memories,
the weed pulling and the watering that began this garden.
The farmer in me answers, "Life, it is life that grows in a garden."

—REVEREND DR. JACK E. SKILES

MY BELOVED

The Earth is my Mother.
The wind is my Mother's breath.
Trees, flowers, birds and animals—
all are my beloved Mother.

The waves are my Mother's cheeks,
the stones my Mother's feet.
Trees, flowers, birds and animals—
all are my beloved Mother.

The stars are my Mother's crown,
the sun and moon my Mother's eyes.
Trees, flowers, birds and animals—
all are my beloved Mother.

—JANINE CANAN

WEED WRESTLING

There's something quite healing about
squatting
down into soil,
digging deep with trowel or
gloved hands,
pulling out wild invaders
of our garden patch.

Sometimes,
they protest too much,
grab hold of each other
so tightly
that extra human effort is needed
to rid them
from their tentacled nest.

Other gardeners might complain,
but for me,
this is a prescription for mental health,
removing all the pains and problems past
with each volatile pull.

At end of another day of weed wrestling,
my back may hurt, my shoulders complain,
but the hassles of a harried life
are somehow lessened
by this therapeutic tug-of-war.

—SUSAN ROGERS NORTON

WATCHING FROM THE WINDOW

My oldest friend, an invalid in her 50s, stands at her kitchen window to watch me mulch her roses one winter morning. The next thing I know, she is at my elbow in her slippers.

"My dear, go back inside. You'll catch cold!"

"I just had to tell you something," she said. "One of my elderly friends told me that, when she could no longer garden, she watched a younger friend do for her what you're doing for me. As I watched you from the window over my sink, I felt the smiling shadows of all the women who have nurtured gardens for friends so they can enjoy their flowers a little longer."

So true. I divided daylilies for my aging grandmother, buried bulbs for my bone-weary mother, and, one spring, I cleaned flowerbeds for a friend who could see her perennial border from her deathbed. We tend our own gardens and those of others because gardens grow in hearts as well as soil, now and forever. Amen.

—MARTHA K. BAKER

SWEET BANQUETS

You don't have to own
your neighbor's garden
to enjoy its flowers
and even the eyes of strangers
may feast upon the sweet banquets
of someone else's work.

—HILDA LACHNEY SANDERSON

THE SHADY CORNER

I park my child's wagon
in "The Shady Corner"
of the Botanical Garden
and fill it with old
favorites from the woods
and its dank borders:

Solomon's Seal, Lily
of the Valley, American ginger,
Dutchman's Breeches,
Rhineland astilbe; freckled violet,
bleeding heart, bloodroot,
and Sweet Woodruff;

creamy yellow wild columbine
and blessed Lenten
and Christmas roses—

such silent grace
might inspire even
the staunchest of infidels
to bedrock faith.

After the crippling frost
of a demonic winter
I pull my wagonful
of balm for the spirit
across the shadows

pause in the sun to pay
my debt at a table before
the gate of the garden

and drive away inhaling
the essence of woods
to transplant my faith
with my fingers into
the shadows around
the corners of my home.

—NORBERT KRAPF

IN THE GARDEN

We name the world—we name the things in the world—in order to
know it: see it. My daughter points and says, "Coat, shoes, dog, flower,"
and by doing so she places herself in the world: places herself among
the things that make up her world.

When I take her to see the mid-spring beginnings of my grand-
dad's garden—the invisible growing underneath the soil, the unborn
turning over in the belly of the earth—we stand by his side and watch
him point his bones-twisted-with-arthritis fingers at seeds that are
still waiting to break ground. We listen to his voice—his Hungarian
tongue—tell us, give us, the litany of plant names, as if he is listing the
root names growing out from our family tree: green beans, Hungarian
pepper, tomatoes, paprika, sunflowers, corn. He speaks like a man
with faith: faith that the earth, if properly tended to and cared for, will
continue to give rise to new growth: to a new generation of branches
and leaves.

Helena is the newborn keeper of our family garden. She shall
inherit more than just the earth.

—PETER MARKUS

WHY DO PLANTS HAVE SUCH A POSITIVE IMPACT ON US?

Why do plants have such a positive impact on us? There are a number of reasons, including: They have a predictable cycle of life that provides comfort in our time of rapid change. They are responsive but nonthreatening. They form no opinions or judgments about their caregivers. They soften our man-made environment. They enable us to change or improve our environment. They promote relaxation and tranquility.

—AUTHOR UNKNOWN

WORKING IN THE GARDEN

When jasmine sprawls over the fence, seductive
as a languid woman, I am pleased.
And when narcissi send up slender stalks,
but no luscious flowers, I'm disappointed.
But if one fails, the other thrives. Nature
is like that. It doesn't care. This seed
lands in fertile soil, the sun, the rain is right.
It grows to a sapling, then madrone,
limbs bronzed as children by the sea all summer.
That another lands on rock or is washed away
or sprouts and is trampled, doesn't matter.
Nature wants life, but any life will do.
I stay outside till dark, hashing up the ground.
Inside is my daughter. She has split
the hard shell of her seed
and a lone naked root is searching the soil.
I don't even know what she needs.
Anything I offer—or withhold—
may be wrong. And she can't tell me.
She is mute as a plant. And so individual,
like the bean I grew in a jar in third grade,
my own bean, the tiny white hairs of its root
delicate as the fuzz on a newborn's crown.
Just a singular seed and the treacherous odds.

—ELLEN BASS

DO TELL

Each flower holds a story: Do tell.

Mother babied the night-blooming day lily, these black iris, and
     that spirea.
I started this hosta from one in the village commonspace (a
     midnight "harvest").
The flowering almond's powder-puff blooms lined Grandmother's
     rural walk.
The fuzzy deutzia belonged to my friend, who didn't even know its
     name.

The white peony, too. The pink peony grew in my other
     grandmother's city bed.
The little dogwood arrived after the old redbuds crashed through
     the electric wires.
My husband gave me the fountains of Miscanthus grasses for our
     fourth anniversary.
A moving neighbor donated her butterfly bushes; the butterflies
     piggybacked along.

Each plant says a prayer: Live on.

—MARTHA K. BAKER

AT THE END OF A SEASON

There's a bucket of radishes against the fence,
a box of golden potatoes set down beside the back door;
half-green tomato vines he'd brought in to ripen
in the old shed, shielded from the first frost.

A hoe, an old rusty shovel, leaned against
the barn wall, and two worn lawn chairs
he always said he'd reweave one day,
tucked into one another.

His old straw hat on a hook, waiting.

—MARILYN JOHNSTON

ten

INSPIRATION

A garden is a living symbol of optimism, proof that patience has its rewards and confirmation that tender loving care cultivates beauty.

—VERONICA HUNSUCKER

SHORT INSPIRATIONS

The earth is a large garden, and each of us need only care for our own part for life to be breathed back into the planet, into the soil, into ourselves.

—JOHN JEAVONS

In my room, my prayers are not so frequent or so fervent; but, at the sight of a beautiful landscape, I feel myself moved without knowing why.

—JEAN-JACQUES ROUSSEAU (1712–1778)

A garden really lives only insofar as it is an expression of faith,
the embodiment of a hope and a song of praise.

—RUSSELL PAGE

BE A GARDENER

Be a gardener.
Dig a ditch,
toil and sweat,
and turn the earth upside down
and seek the deepness
and water the plants in time.
Continue this labor
and make sweet floods to run
and noble and abundant fruits
to spring.
Take this food and drink
and carry it to God
as your true worship.

—JULIAN OF NORWICH (1342–CA.1416)

BLESSING FOR A GARDENER

May you work within earth's plenty,
befriend more than you can see.

May you discover life's hidden bounty,
feast on its sumptuous fare.

May what you touch be blessed,
and what you touch bless you.

May your garden grow all season
to fill your heart all year.

—MARYANNE HANNAN

GIVE ME THE SPLENDID SILENT SUN

Give me the splendid silent sun with all his beams full-dazzling,

Give me autumnal fruit ripe and red from the orchard,

Give me a field where the unmow'd grass grows,

Give me an arbor, give me the trellis'd grape,

Give me fresh corn and wheat, give me serene-moving animals
teaching content,

Give me nights perfectly quiet as on high plateaus west of the
Mississippi, and I looking up at the stars,

Give me odorous at sunrise a garden of beautiful flowers where I can
walk undisturb'd.

—WALT WHITMAN (1819–1892)

PILGRIM'S PROGRESS

At the gate that guides red roses upward
In their winging,
Peace holds me like a hymn's half-note
That fills with singing.

My luggage only garden tools—
Grass clippers, weeder.
I stop to watch a hummingbird
Bound for its feeder.

At beds of crimson, yellow, white,
Clear sky my ceiling,
I make a tasseled shadow there,
In light stay kneeling.

—IDA FASEL (1909–2012)

LET US GIVE THANKS

Let us give thanks for a bounty of people.

For children who are our second planting, and though they grow like weeds and the wind too soon blows them away, may they forgive us our cultivation and fondly remember where their roots are.

Let us give thanks:

For generous friends with hearts as big as hubbards and smiles as bright as their blossoms.

For feisty friends as tart as apples;

For continuous friends, who, like scallions and cucumbers, keep reminding us that we've had them;

For crotchety friends, as sour as rhubarb and as indestructible;

For handsome friends, who are as gorgeous as eggplants and as elegant as a row of corn, and the others, as plain as potatoes and as good for you;

For funny friends, who are as silly as Brussels sprouts and as amusing as Jerusalem artichokes, and serious friends, as complex as cauliflowers and as intricate as onions;

For friends as unpretentious as cabbage, as subtle as summer squash, as persistent as parsley, as delightful as dill, as endless as zucchini, and who, like parsnips, can be counted on to see you through the winter;

For old friends, nodding like sunflowers in the evening-time, and young friends coming on as fast as radishes;

For loving friends, who wind around us like tendrils and hold us, despite our blights, wilts and witherings;

And finally, for those friends now gone, like gardens past that have been harvested, and who fed us in their times that we might have life thereafter;

For all these we give thanks.

—REVEREND MAX ALDEN COOTS (1927–2009)

WHEN I DANCE, I DANCE

When I dance, I dance, when I sleep, I sleep; yes, and when I walk alone in a beautiful orchard, if my thoughts drift to far-off matters for some part of the time, for some other part I lead them back again to the walk, the orchard, to the sweetness of this solitude, to myself.

—MICHEL DE MONTAIGNE (1533–1592)

A LITTLE PRAYER

Send, O God...
A little sun,
A little shower,
A tiny seed,
A garden flower.

—THERESA MARY GRASS

THE SIMPLEST MIRACLE

From humble soil
and seeds so unassuming
to the joy, of those first few shoots

How did the small green leaves
straining toward the sun…
misted with rain
develop into these innocent
beautiful blossoms?

How can the miracle of a pumpkin,
a squash
or a pepper
occur?

In a world filled with doubt
step into a garden
to know
Divine intervention
exists.

—MARY MAUDE DANIELS

GARDEN CREDO

I believe in Gaia the Mother All-tender,
Earth Spirit, maker of gardens,
and in her sons and daughters,
the trees and plants of four seasons.
I believe in the white lilies
and red ranunculus of summer,
and in their seeds.
I believe in the pears and apples of autumn,
the pumpkins, the blue-gray squashes
that nourish our bodies with their meat,
our spirits with their beauty.
I believe in the holly of winter
whose needling leaves and red berries
unite the green of Gaia to the blood of Christ.
I believe in the crocus and tulips of spring
whose petals open like sacred chalices
from which all may drink the joy of the garden.

—THELMA J. PALMER

GARDEN BLESSING

Thanks be to God
for diverse seasons,
the flowers and trees,
the seeds and the weeds,
the stillness and breeze,
the showers and the sun,
nature old and young,
all that's cold or hot:
Thanks be to God.

—SHIRLEY VOGLER MEISTER

ILLUMINATION

A break in the storm, hosanna
opal light floods the garden, writes
flames of cedar waxwings
whistling in the sycamore,
sun-clad cats lounging
in riches of tender weed,
silken whirring of a hummingbird
needling a drowsy mallow,
the clappers of calla lily tongues
clanging golden incense in the sun.
Let this beauty be its own prayer
gilded on the air's new skin.

—SARAH J. DIEHL

A GARDENER'S PRAYER

Gentle Mother Nature,
let me learn the lessons
that my garden has to show
today and every day.

Teach me the faith of bumblebees
who buzz from bloom to bloom,
defying all of science
to fly on belief alone.

Teach me the hope of seeds and bulbs.
Though buried deep in darkness,
they trust in the light and wait—
patient and sure of rising.

Teach me the love of all green things,
who give us their beauty and scent,
bless us with fruit and shade,
and want nothing in return.

—NANCY PRIFF

HEIRLOOM SEEDS

Treasured heirloom seeds
passed lovingly
with care and respect
throughout the generations...
Nature's enduring tribute
to the value and worth
of all that remains...
...and all that is yet to be.

—CINDY CHUKSUDOON

THE GARDENER'S TOAST

May your garden have lilies;
your window a view.
May your barn have an owl
and your lovers be true.

May your fences be friendly,
have gates, no barbed-wire.
May your smoke-house stand tall
and never catch fire.

May your apple trees bear
luscious fruit without scab,
and your pots in the sea
fill with Dungeness crab.

May your dogs never chase
after black cows or cars,
and your nights never be
without candles or stars.

May you always have one or two
bucks in your pockets,
and friends, on the Fourth,
who like picnics and rockets.

May the watercress grow
lush and green in your creek.
May your well overflow,
and your roof never leak.

—THELMA J. PALMER

A COMMUNITY GARDEN BLESSING

Let us direct our desire for a better world
into the earth itself.
Each seed we plant, however small,
is a tangible wish for growth:
for shoots of tenderness,
for roots of extending kindness.
And may the greenest, most hopeful leaves
be lessons of compassion
taken from our holiest books.

—CAROL L. MACKAY

PLOWING A NEW FURROW

How shortsighted we are, Gardener of our souls, when we don't look past our drained, sprayed, rolled and manicured lawns to Your intricate balance of nature. Teach us reverence for all creation, for we're walking with roughshod boots over everything in sight, calling it progress. Restrain our heavy hands on pesticides, pond drainers, pollution pumps, paving machines. We've not yet gotten the picture that all things work together for good, from worms that become butterflies, plants that heal and streams that quench. Reconnect us to soil and sea from whence we came and will return; remind us how earthy we are!

—MARGARET ANNE HUFFMAN (1941–2000)

BEATITUDES FOR THE GARDENER

Blessed are the weeds, for they prove my garden soil is fruitful, and all that weeding keeps my waist trim.

Blessed are the birds, for they remind me to share and to bury some seeds deeper so they can't get at them.

Blessed are the slugs and snails, for they remind me that there is a plan for all creatures, great and small, and my chickens love to snack on them.

Blessed are the ants, for they remind me to be industrious and not to leave my lunch on the garden seat.

Blessed are the crickets, for they drown out the creaking of my aging joints.

Blessed is my neighbor's fruit tree, for the windfalls land on my side of the fence.

Blessed is even my neighbor's walking bamboo, for it makes useful garden stakes when I chop it down.

Blessed is my garden in the early morning, when the dew is fresh and sparkling, and I remembered to protect my seedlings from frost.

Blessed is my garden in the afternoon, when my garden is a haven of peace and a retreat from my busy day.

Blessed is my garden in the evening, when I am thankful for family and friends and the scent of jasmine.

Blessed is my compost heap, because it saves me having to get a dog to clean up the kitchen scraps.

Blessed is my dog, which followed the kids home and moved in anyway.

Blessed are my well worn and much loved gardening tools that have never let me down.

Blessed is Christmas, when everyone buys me new gardening tools.

Blessed is Spring, when new life fills my garden and my heart fills with joy.

Blessed is Summer, when the bees hum, the air is sweet with the scent of flowers and I garden in a shady hat.

Blessed is Autumn, when I harvest the fruits of my garden, and have to make enough pickled zucchini to feed an army.

Blessed is Winter, when I curl up by the fire with my seed catalogs and plan for Spring.

Blessed is the rain, that falls like manna from Heaven and brings my garden to life—and gets me pulling those darn weeds again.

Blessed is the sun, which always comes out when I have lost my gardening hat.

Blessed is my gardening hat, which I finally found in the dog's kennel.

Blessed are those cool, balmy days when the flowers are blooming and the vegetables are thriving and I know it is all worthwhile.

Blessed is the person who told me to mulch because I finally can get a handle on those darn weeds.

And most blessed is the great Gardener, who made all the earth to be our garden.

—GAIL KAVANAGH

KEEPER OF THE GATES

Keeper of the gates,
we thank you for being husband to the earth,
mother to every creature,
caretaker of every flower
and every grain of wheat.

—FATHER JOHN B. GIULIANI

MIRACLE

The gift
of the gardener
is that
she holds promise
in her hands
and faith
in her heart.

—THERESA MARY GRASS

A GARDEN PRAYER

what the moon says, change
what the sun says, burn
what the ground says, plant
what the flower says, praise
what the grass says, dance
what the willow says, yield
what the rooster says, sing
what the wind says, play
what God says, be

—MARIAN OLSON

GOD'S EVERGREENNESS

Holy One of Glory,

You bless me with the beauty
Of green, growing grasses
And pink, blooming roses,
Of screaming-yellow glads
And spicy, rusted marigolds.
You bless me with the hard work
Of tilling the stone-filled soil
And digging the rooted earth,
Of weeding the planted beds
And pinching dead blossoms.
You bless me with the renewal
Of daffodils on the first of May
And daylilies under summer's sun,
Of chrysanthemums in Autumn chill
And Lenten roses long past winter.
You bless me with unending desire
For the strengthening of the good work
And the chance to share the loveliness,
For the enfolding flowers themselves
And the evergreenness of Your love.

—MARTHA K. BAKER

GARDEN PRAYER

Let the soil receive these plantings
and cradle them in sweet fertility.
Let the rain fall softly
and the sun smile down,
coaxing each seed and sprout
into lavish growth and blossom.
Let creatures of earth and air find welcome here,
adding their different voices and vibrant colors
to the perfumed landscape.
Let this be a place of harmony,
of peace and rejuvenation for the spirit.
Let us tend this garden
with joy and reverence
so that it will reflect—like a small mirror—
the Beauty of all Creation.

—SHARON HUDNELL

BLESS THE GARDENER

May the good Lord bless the gardener,
And his hand that holds the seed;
May he have the strength to kneel
And to gently pull each weed.

May the good Lord bless the gardener,
Whose devotion never ends;
For he sprinkles love and patience
On each flower that he tends.

May the good Lord bless the gardener,
For the task he does so well;
For the beauty and the fragrance
In each rose we stop to smell.

May the good Lord bless the gardener,
As he plants his seeds each spring;
For he made the Master happy,
And he made the Angels sing.

—KAY MCCARTHY REALL

GARDEN LIGHT

Let us seek to paint what we experience here...
not in detail, but broad brush strokes

capturing sunlight and the shadows that lace
the gravel paths, the grass,

the flowers, radiant in their beds,
and the sky, its white clouds drifting against the blue.

Everything as it is, insists on itself:
the song birds, the owls, the lady bugs,

each a reminder of this opportunity
for adoration, for doing and saying nothing,

for embracing, as we might,
the generous gift of this garden light.

—MICHAEL S. GLASER

Author Index

Permissions and Acknowledgments

Grateful acknowledgment is made to the authors and publishers for the use of the following material. Every effort has been made to contact original sources. If notified, the publishers will be pleased to rectify an omission in future editions.

Martha K. Baker for "Do Tell," "God's Evergreenness," and "Watching from the Window."

Ellen Bass for "Working in the Garden" from *Mules of Love*. Copyright © 2002 by Ellen Bass. Reprinted with the permission of The Permissions Company, Inc., on behalf of BOA Editions Ltd. www.boaeditions.org, www.ellenbass.com

Tereasa Bellew for "The Garden." www.tereasa-thingfinder.blogspot.com

Heather Berry for "Glory to the Gardener."

Gwyneth M. Bledsoe for "A Hummingbird Moment." www.gwynethbledsoe.com

Mike Blottenberger for "Leaves Falling."

Ann Reisfeld Boutté for "The Visit."

Gayle Brandeis for "Avocado" and "Choking." www.gaylebrandeis.com

Susanne Wiggins Bunch for "A Gardener's Lament."

Pamela Burke for "A Gardener Knows Another Gardener."

Meg Campbell for "Lilies."

Janine Canan for "Honored Bees," "Lovely Camellia," and "My
Beloved." www.janinecanan.com

Cindy Chuksudoon for "Heirloom Seeds."

Jill Morgan Clark for "Bumble Bees in Bloom."

Sally Clark for "Kindness." www.sallyclark.info

Roddy O'Neil Cleary for "A Gardener's Springtime Prayer" by William
Cleary.

Ginny Lowe Connors for "Holy Tomatoes." www.ginnyloweconnors.com

Barbara Crooker for "Diminuendo," "Flowering Trees," "January
Thaw," "Late February," "Raspberries," "Suddenly," "This Summer
Day," and "Turning the Garden Under." www.barbaracrooker.com

Mary Maude Daniels for "Fall Bounty" and "The Simplest Miracle."

Dianne M. Del Giorno for "Old Gardener's Confession."

Denise A. DeWald for "All Because Autumn Came."

Sarah J. Diehl for "Illumination."

Susan J. Erickson for "Gardening Credo."

Finishing Line Press for "Affair in a Garden" by Arlene Gay Levine.
Copyright © 2011 by Arlene Gay Levine. Published in *Movie Life*
(Finishing Line Press). Used with permission from Finishing Line
Press. www.finishinglinepress.com, www.arlenegaylevine.com

Maureen Tolman Flannery for "Katydid" and "Their Garden."

Nancy Lynch Gibson for "Buried Treasure" and "The Old Gardener."

Father John B. Giuliani for "Keeper of the Gates."

Michael S. Glaser for "Garden Light" and "Making Soup for Selah."
www.michaelsglaser.com

Barbara J. Glynn for "August Clearing."

Theresa Mary Grass for "A Blessing for a Gardener," "A Little Prayer,"
and "Miracle."

Maryanne Hannan for "Blessing for a Gardener" and "Ground."
www.mhannan.com

Me Hansburg for "Liturgy."

Bonnie Compton Hanson for "Snowflakes of Spring."
www.bonniecomptonhanson.com

Penny Harter for "Shelling Peas." www.2hweb.net/penhart

C. David Hay for "The Wilding."

Rochelle Lynn Holt for "Flowers."

Sharon Hudnell for "Cycle: for the Deer," "Garden Prayer," and "The
New Garden."

Gary W. Huffman for "Plowing a New Furrow" by Margaret Anne
Huffman.

Hazel Smith Hutchinson for "Contractions." www.ArtEnSoulCollage.com

Anita Jepson-Gilbert for "Pilgrim's Progress" by Ida Fasel.

Jill McCabe Johnson for "Child's Garden Blessing" and "Garden
Confessional." www.jillmccabejohnson.com

Marilyn Johnston for "At the End of a Season."

Gail Kavanagh for "Beatitudes for the Gardener."
www.gailkavanagh.wordpress.com

Joanne Keaton for "Year-Round Blessing."

Emily King for "Lady Autumn." www.emilyking.net

Paula E. Kirman for "Gardening Mother" and "Winter Blessing."
www.mynameispaula.com

Brenda Knight for "Four O'clocks."

Norbert Krapf for "Morning Glories" and "The Shady Corner."
www.krapfpoetry.com

Susan Landon for "Harvest Time."

Fanny Levin for "The Rose."

Arlene Gay Levine for "A Gardener's Prayer." www.arlenegaylevine.com

Nancy Tupper Ling for "What Remains." www.nancytupperling.com

Katharyn Howd Machan for "Grandmother."

Carol L. MacKay for "A Community Garden Blessing" and "Into a
Bountiful Season."

Arlene L. Mandell for "Gardener's Winter Lament."

Peter Markus for "The Earth Turns Green" and "In the Garden."

Barb Mayer for "Discovery." www.barbmayer.com

Sandra E. McBride for "A Poet's Prayer" and "Why?"

Gary E. McCormick for "Making the Rounds."

Shirley Vogler Meister for "Garden Blessing."

Sheryl L. Nelms for "Grandma and Grandpa's Backyard," "Leap Frog,"
and "Your Flowers Are Pretty." www.pw.org/content/sheryl_l_nelms

Joan Noëldechen for "The Promise."

Susan Rogers Norton for "Weed Wrestling."

Barbara Nuzzo for "A Garden Blessing."

William Orem for "Tomato." www.williamorem.com

Thelma J. Palmer for "Garden Credo," "Gardens," and "The Gardener's Toast."

Nita Penfold for "And They Say There Are No More." www.nitapenfold.com

Jeani M. Picklesimer for "Rhapsodies Within."

Nancy Priff for "A Gardener's Prayer."

Mary Lenore Quigley for "The Gardener." www.q2ink.com

Charlotte C. Ramsay for "Let Us Give Thanks" by Reverend Max Alden Coots. Published in *View from a Tree*. Copyright © 1989 by Reverend Max Alden Coots. Published by MRS Printing and Publishing, Inc.

Steven Ratiner for "Early Daffodils."

Kay McCarthy Reall for "Bless the Gardener."

DeMar Regier for "Garden Gift."

Thomas L. Reid for "Summer Passing" and "To Marigolds in Autumn."

Elisavietta Ritchie for "Your Gift of Tomatoes." www.elisaviettaandclyde.com

Zoraida Rivera Morales for "Garden Talk."

Marjorie Rommel for "Orchard Blessing."

Helen Ruggieri for "Warts."

Linda Lee Ruzicka for "Dawn Approaches."

Hilda Lachney Sanderson for "Sweet Banquets."

Marion Schoeberlein for "The Butterfly Ballet" and "Trees."

Mary Kolada Scott for "Bless the Gardener Who." www.marykoladascott.com

Irene Sedeora for "Oasis."

Stephanie B. Shafran for "Morning Glories."

Sherri Waas Shunfenthal for "Eden."

Reverend Dr. Jack E. Skiles for "Curator."

Snapshot Press for "A Garden Prayer," by Marian Olson, originally titled "From a Morning Meditation." Published in *Consider This*. Copyright © 2012 Marian Olson. Published by Snapshot Press. www.snapshotpress.co.uk/ebooks.htm

Laurence Snydal for "Garden."

Molly Srode for "Morning's Gift."

Cassie Premo Steele for "Squash Blossom." www.cassiepremosteele.com

Joan Stephen for "Psalm of Praise."

Shirley S. Stevens for "Spring Pledge."

Lois Greene Stone for "Natural."

Ramnath Subramanian for "The Garden Warbler."

Robin M. Svedi for "My Garden's Protected." www.seasonalshowers.com

Christine Swanberg for "The Garden Hour."

bg Thurston for "A Poet Returns to the Garden."

Lisa Timpf for "Spring Raking."

Jean Tupper for "Love Poem for the Gardener." www.finelinepoets.com

Barbara J. Van Noord for "Blessings."

Donna Wahlert for "Birds at the Feeder" and "In the Garden with My Grandson."

Reverend Edie Weinstein for "The Gardener." www.liveinjoy.org

Norman Wirzba for "Spiritual Gardening," excerpted from *Food and Faith: A Theology of Eating*. Copyright © 2011 by Norman Wirzba. Published by Cambridge University Press. Used with permission from Norman Wirzba.

http://divinity.duke.edu/academics/faculty/norman-wirzba

Rebecca K. Wyss for "Cricket's Coda."

Gary Young for "It's Early Winter."

Lisa Zimmerman for "Pear Tree at Sunset."

About the Author

JUNE COTNER is the author and editor of twenty-eight books, including the best-selling *Graces, Bedside Prayers,* and *Dog Blessings.* Her books altogether have sold nearly one million copies.

June's latest love and avocation is giving presentations on "Adopting Prisoner-Trained Shelter Dogs." In 2011, she adopted Indy, a chocolate Lab/Doberman mix (a LabraDobie!), from the Freedom Tails program at Stafford Creek Corrections Center in Aberdeen, Washington. June works with Indy daily to build on the wonderful obedience skills he mastered in the program. She and Indy have appeared on the television shows *AM Northwest* (Portland, OR) and *New Day Northwest* (Seattle).

A graduate of the University of California at Berkeley, June is the mother of two grown children and lives in Poulsbo, Washington with her husband. Her hobbies include yoga, hiking, paper crafting, and playing with her two grandchildren.

For more information, please visit June's website at www.junecotner.com.

Author photograph by Barb Mayer Photography

TO OUR READERS

Viva Editions publishes books that inform, enlighten, and entertain. We do our best to bring you, the reader, quality books that celebrate life, inspire the mind, revive the spirit, and enhance lives all around. Our authors are practical visionaries: people who offer deep wisdom in a hopeful and helpful manner. Viva was launched with an attitude of growth and we want to spread our joy and offer our support and advice where we can to help you live the Viva way: vivaciously!

We're grateful for all our readers and want to keep bringing you books for inspired living. We invite you to write to us with your comments and suggestions, and what you'd like to see more of. You can also sign up for our online newsletter to learn about new titles, author events, and special offers.

Viva Editions
2246 Sixth St.
Berkeley, CA 94710
www.vivaeditions.com
(800) 780-2279
Follow us on Twitter @vivaeditions
Friend/fan us on Facebook